CLARENCE E. MACARTNEY

HE CHOSE
TWELVE

Other Books by Clarence E. Macartney
Twelve Great Questions About Christ
Great Women of the Bible
Paul the Man
The Greatest Texts of the Bible
He Chose Twelve

CLARENCE E. MACARTNEY

HE CHOSE
TWELVE

kregel PUBLICATIONS
Grand Rapids, MI 49501

He Chose Twelve, by Clarence Edward Macartney, © 1993
by Kregel Publications, a division of Kregel, Inc., P.O. Box
2607, Grand Rapids, Michigan, 49501. All rights reserved

Cover and Book Design: Alan G. Hartman

Library of Congress Cataloging-in-Publication Data

Macartney, Clarence Edward Noble, 1879-1957.
[Of them He chose twelve]
He chose twelve / Clarence Edward Macartney.
     p.   cm.
  Originally published: Of them he chose twelve.
Philadelphia : Dorrance and Company, 1927.
  1. Apostles. I. Title.
BS2440.M25   1993   225.9'22—dc20   92-23989
                                             CIP

ISBN 0-8254-3270-7

          1 2 3 4 5 year / printing 97 96 95 94 93

CONTENTS

INTRODUCTION

A number of years ago I purchased from an unfortunate art dealer a copy of Leonardo da Vinci's Last Supper. It was more compassion for the broken and aged dealer than love for this kind of art that moved me to make the purchase, although I had every reason to accept the high judgment which he passed on the picture. When I had secured the picture it became a problem of disposition rather than a subject for admiration, its dimensions rendering it out of place in any ordinary room or study. At length I shipped it to my old home in Pennsylvania and hung it on the wall of the dining room.

During a long stay at home one summer, I frequently examined the painting and began to appreciate for the first time its great excellence and to understand how this work of da Vinci's became so famous. A casual and occasional glance let me see just twelve men of flowing robes and Hebraic cast of countenance sitting at table with their Master. But continued and repeated observation began to reveal more than a mere group of thirteen men, very much alike. I began to see the individuality, the personality of each member of the group: the clutching avarice of Judas, the dreamy mysticism of Bartholomew, the burning zeal of Simon, the impulsive aggressiveness of Peter and the despairing melancholy of Thomas.

Our general and casual reading of the New Testament may be likened to a careless glance at the Italian's masterpiece, for we see a number of men and do not mark much difference between them. The careful study of the New Testament reveals more than that; it rewards us by making each one of the Twelve Disciples stand out in his own personality and individuality. It is indeed true that of some of the disciples we know hardly anything, but even when their name in a catalogue of the Twelve is all that we have to go by, it is possible to frame a distinct conception of each of the twelve men chosen by Christ to build the church upon the foundation which He Himself had laid. In one of his essays, William Hazlitt speaks of Charles Lamb and some of his friends discussing the question of persons they would like to have known. Lamb dismisses Sir Isaac Newton and William Locke, stars of the first magnitude, because, although distinguished and notable for their achievements, they were not characters, not real persons. "Yes, the greatest names, but they were not persons, not persons." This study of the Twelve Disciples will not have been in vain if it shall result in taking these twelve men out from their hiding place between the covers of the Bible and making them live before us as interesting and, in the Providence of God, mighty personalities, humble and unlearned, it is true, but nevertheless human forces acting at the sources of Christian history and, therefore, mighty agents of destiny.

But there are reasons other than those of mere curiosity or biographical interest. The four men who wrote the Gospels bearing their names were not, it is to be remembered, writing biographical sketches of the disciples of Christ. The Great Personality about whom they are thinking and writing is Christ. Whatever they tell us of Peter, John, Andrew and the rest is but incidental to the story of the Son Himself about whom these lesser lights cluster. It is the study of these men that compels us to study the Master who had chosen them out of the world to witness for Him before men. We cannot earnestly and prayerfully study the lives and characters of the Twelve Apostles without coming to a better understanding of the mission, and a clearer vision of the glorious character of Him who spent most of the time of His ministry upon earth in training the Twelve by precept, by example, by love and patience, by warning and rebuke, by miracle and by daily companionship. Despite temptations and temporary lapses, the disciples, as a body, remained true to Christ and the work He had given them to do. This magnificent fidelity was based upon complete confidence in the Person of Jesus, and that confidence was possible only because of their intimacy with Him. If we know the Apostles better we shall be rewarded by knowing better Him whom to know aright is Eternal Life. In the words of one of the chief students in this fascinating field, A. B. Bruce, the author of *The Training of the Twelve* [1], "All, therefore, who desire to get the benefit of this trust, must be willing to spend time and take the trouble to get into the heart of the Gospel story, and of its great subject.

"The sure anchorage is not attainable by a listless, random reading of the evangelistic narratives, but by a close, careful, prayerful study, pursued, it may be, for years. Those who grudge the trouble are in imminent danger of the fate which befell the ignorant multitude, being liable to be thrown into panic by every new infidel book, or to be scandalized by every strange utterance of the object of faith. Those, on the other hand, who do take the trouble will be rewarded for their pains. Storm-tossed for a time, they shall at length reach the harbor of creed which is no nondescript compromise between infidelity and Scriptural Christianity, but embraces all the cardinal facts and truths of the faith as taught by Jesus."

In John's great vision of the holy city, the New Jerusalem, which had the glory of God, he tells us that the twelve gates of the city were inscribed with the names of the twelve tribes of Israel, but that the twelve foundations of the city were engraved with the twelve names of the Apostles of the Lamb. If the names of the twelve tribes of Israel on the gates of the city suggest the completeness of the company of the saved and the fullness of redemption, the names of the Twelve Apostles of the Lamb graven on the twelve foundations remind us that upon the foundation which they laid in Jesus Christ was builded the whole vast structure of Christian history. Therefore it is that their names live forever.

---

1. A. B. Bruce, *The Training of the Twelve*, published by Kregel Publications, Grand Rapids, Michigan 49501

PUBLISHER'S PREFACE

Clarence Edward Noble Macartney (1879-1957) ministered in Paterson, New Jersey, and Philadelphia, Pennsylvania, before assuming the influential pastorate of First Presbyterian Church, Pittsburgh, Pennsylvania, where he ministered for twenty-seven years.

His preaching especially attracted men, not only to the Sunday services but also to his popular Tuesday noon luncheons. He was gifted in dealing with Bible biographies, and, in this respect, has well been called "the American Alexander Whyte." The biographical sketches in this book represent some of his best preaching. Dr. Cyril Barber in *The Minister's Library* says they are ". . . indispensable studies of the apostles." It is a pleasure and a privelege to reissue this worthy book!

1

ANDREW

Andrew was always bringing someone to Jesus. He brought his brother, Peter; he brought the lad with the barley loaves and the two fishes; he brought the inquiring Greeks.

With the mention of Andrew begins the long day of Christian history. Obscure are the beginnings of nations and systems and men. Not less so were the beginnings of the Christian Church. John was beyond Jordan baptizing. It was the second day after he had baptized Jesus. John and two of his disciples were standing by the roadside when Jesus passed by. As He passed, John exclaimed, "Behold the Lamb of God!" One of the two disciples was Andrew (John 1:40), and he with his companion, in all probability John, having heard what John the Baptist had said about Jesus, turned to follow Him. With that turning begins Christian history, Christian discipleship. What if Andrew and his companion had not turned! That act on their part was like a pebble on yonder mountain ridge which obstructs the rain that has fallen and turns it to the east or to the west, to the north or to the south. So from the heights of will and desire, the will and the desire of Andrew and his unnamed but not unknown companion, descended the stream of Christian history.

A DISCIPLE OF JOHN THE BAPTIST

Andrew's antecedents are good. He appears first in the sacred narrative as a disciple of John the Baptist. That meant that he appreciated spiritual values, that the mighty proclamation of the Baptist about repentance and judgment and the Kingdom of God found response in his fisherman's heart. The synoptic evangelists make no mention of the first meeting between Christ and the men who were to become His disciples. But John treasures it among his most sacred memories, and after the sublime introduction to his Gospel he relates that casual, apparently insignificant, meeting when Andrew and he turned to follow One whom they had heard the Baptist describe as the Lamb of God.

They who seek always find. Jesus, seeing them following, knowing all that was in their hearts, said to them, "What seek ye?" They said unto Him, "Master, where dwellest Thou?" He said unto them, "Come and see." They came and saw where He dwelt, and abode with Him that day; for it was about the tenth hour. What they talked about during that visit we do not know. "Something sealed the lips of that evangelist." But the result was that Andrew, at least, went away convinced that Jesus was the Messiah, the Christ. On our dull ears today that announcement falls like a commonplace. It awakens no thrill of hope or expectation. But with Andrew it was different. The devout Hebrew knew the voices and signs and promises of the past about Israel's coming Redeemer, the Prince of Peace, the Mighty Counselor, the Dayspring from on high, the Desire of the nations, the Star out of Jacob and the Scepter out of Israel. A few hours in the company of a strange young man on the other side Jordan, and Andrew was convinced that Jesus was the Christ.

Millions have believed on Jesus as the Christ, the Son of God, the Savior of the world. What a host as they pass by in review, called out of every nation and tribe and kindred and people and tongue, out of every age—the men, the women, the little children! They have believed in Jesus and have worshipped Him and prayed to Him as Christ. At the head of that glorious procession comes Andrew, the first fruits of the world, his lips the first to frame the accents of faith, his confession the first note in that chorus which is to grow in volume from age to age and which this day makes heaven and earth ring with its Te Deum of praise—"Thou art the everlasting Son of the Father, O Christ!"

THE FINAL CONVERT

It meant so much to Andrew, this discovery about Jesus, that he must share it with someone else. With whom? With his own brother, Simon. "He first findeth his own brother Simon, and saith unto him, We have found the Messias, the Christ. And he brought him to Jesus." Incomparable scene that for the beginning of Christianity, Andrew bringing Peter his brother to Jesus! Andrew was not only the first believer, he was the first Christian worker. To him it fell to speak the first good word for Jesus Christ, to bring the first one to Jesus. He is the forerunner of all those who have told people of Christ and have brought others to His feet. For that reason, if there are ranks and distinctions in heaven, I think that not only will the Twelve Apostles seated upon thrones be marked in heaven for their great service to Christ, but Andrew will have about him a peculiar halo as the man who first believed in Christ and brought the first person unto Him.

It said much for the family relationship that it was his own brother to whom Andrew went first of all with the news of the Messiah. It is not difficult to think of families where a man would tell anyone else before he would tell his own brother; sometimes because of animosities and quarreling which make it impossible, even when the heart is full and the mind is earnest, sometimes because of a strange and yet natural hesitancy to speak on these subjects to our own flesh and blood.

"But do you speak with him; I feel that a stranger will have more influence with him than one of his own family." How often is that word spoken to minister or religious worker! It is not normal; it is not the way in which Christianity began to spread in the world. It began to spread by one brother telling another about Christ. It may be that your word for Christ, for God, for the eternal things, spoken to your own flesh and blood, those so near to you that they never expect you to mention the matter to them, will prove to be the word "spoken in season," seed sown upon good soil. It is well to recall the beautiful words of John Keble on St. Andrew in *The Christian Year*:

Who art thou, that wouldst grave thy name
Thus deeply in a brother's heart?
    Look on this saint and learn to frame
Thy love-charm with true Christian art.

First seek thy Savior out, and dwell
Beneath the shadow of His roof,
    Till thou have scanned His features well,
And know Him for the Christ by proof;

Such proof as they are sure to find
Who spend with Him their happy days,
    Clean hands and a self-ruling mind
Ever in tune for love and praise.

Then potent with the spell of heaven
Go, and thine erring brother gain,
    Entice him home to be forgiven,
Till he, too, see his Savior plain.

Or, if before thee in the race,
Urge him with thine advancing tread,
    Till, like twin stars, with even pace,
Each lucid course be duly sped.

No fading, frail memorial give
To soothe his soul when thou art gone,
    But wreaths of hope for aye to live,
And thoughts of good together done.

That so before the judgment-seat,
Though changed and glorified each face,
    Not unremembered ye may meet,
For endless ages to embrace.

We hear little of Andrew after this; on three other occasions only (John 6:1-14; Mark 13:3). But there is no need to tell us anything else. Whatever Andrew may have done during the years with Jesus, or whatever signs and wonders he may have wrought when the power of the Holy Spirit descended upon him at Pentecost, he never did a greater work than when he brought Peter to Christ. Peter is Andrew's claim to greatness. You ask me, What did Andrew do? The answer is, Peter. Men not otherwise noted—plain, steady-going— earnest men, have as a rule been the men who have brought great workers for Christ and the Church into the fold. On a dull winter's day a poor preacher in a London chapel seems to be talking, not to the dozen or so listless hearers on the benches of his chapel, but to a discouraged, perplexed-looking boy on the back seat. The boy was Spurgeon. Here was his Andrew who brought him to Christ. To do this, men must appreciate the true greatness and honor of it, and have it as their heart's verdict that the greatest privilege on earth is to be used of God in bringing unto Him to be reconciled one of His own erring children. "They that be wise shall shine as the brightness of the firmament; and they that turn many to righteousness, as the stars, for ever and ever" (Daniel 12:3). Shine on, faithful Andrew, first to bring a soul to Christ, and let your spirit fall upon us!

Within the Roman Catholic Communion there may be storms and sweeping tides of which we know nothing. But concerning the Protestant Church we do know this of a certainty: that leaders and workers are perplexed and distraught. Take up a copy of a religious journal and you have not read far before you have been told of a score of "problems," "challenges," "dangers," "remedies," "failures." We weary of the discussion at assemblies, conferences, conventions. Old and New Testaments are interpreted in divers fashions, so many that almost any man will find something to his taste or prejudice. Beautiful churches we have, richly endowed colleges and theological seminaries, ornate services, noble organs, earnest ministers. Yet the great lack is so obvious, so apparent that conventions and resolutions and sermons leave it untouched, unspoken. What is it? What but the lack of Andrew's brother-seeking spirit?

TOO FEW ANDREWS

We build, we study, we sing, we pray, we organize; but too seldom do we go. Too few are the Andrews in our midst, in all churches, in the church which we call our home. Christianity cannot grow or flourish or endure or propagate itself because its adherents are able and willing to sing it praises, to defend logically its principles, to live faithfully its precepts, or to state learnedly and eloquently its truths. Nor did it grow and flourish that way. It grew and expanded and influenced the lives of men and nations because it had within its communion men and women who, like Andrew, brought someone else. Give us a race of Andrews in the Church and the gates of hell shall not prevail against it. Give us a race of Andrews in the Church and you will behold a Church rousing herself like a strong man after sleep and shaking her invincible locks.

Give us a race of Andrews and you will see doubts and misgivings and petty questions of order and place and rank consumed by the burning flame of zeal. A few Andrews to act, to really move against this stronghold of Satan bristling with guns of ancient and modern make, will mean more to Christianity than the making of many books by wise scholars or the profound elaboration of Christian doctrine by learned doctors.

People trouble themselves overmuch about recasting Christianity so as to suit the times, which is too often nothing more than an abandonment of what is true and vital and distinctive in Christianity. But that is not the crying need. The crying need is for Andrews, men of conviction, men of faith, men who believe enough about Jesus Christ to make it worth while to tell others, and men who do tell others, who do bring others, who do seek to act for Christ.

It cannot have been so much by great public assemblies, by public worship, although that has ever its great and unassailable place, as by personal contact, conversations in the market place, in the shops and fields, on the ships and in the armies and prisons, one telling another—that the great story was spread throughout the world. How do the new cults, the revived paganisms that masquerade under the name of Christ, spread in our midst today? Through great public meetings, through the words of eloquent protagonists? Not so, but through one telling another. And so the children of this world are wiser in their generation than the children of light.

One of the finest passages in *The Last Days of Pompeii* is that in which Olinthus, lying in the dungeon at the amphitheater, tells his fellow-prisoner, Glaucus, about Christ and the hope of the life to come:

> There was something in this sudden burst of human affection which struck a kindred chord in the soul of the Greek. He felt, for the first time, a sympathy greater than mere affliction between

him and his companion. He crept nearer towards Olinthus; for the Italians, fierce in some points, were not unnecessarily cruel to others; they spared the separate cell and the superfluous chain, and allowed the victims of the arena the sad comfort of such freedom and such companionship as the prison would afford.

"Yes," continued the Christian with holy fervor, "the immortality of the soul—the resurrection, the reunion of the dead—is the great principle of our creed, the great truth a God suffered death itself to attest and proclaim. No fabled Elysium, no poetic Orcus, but a pure and radiant heritage of heaven itself, is the portion of the good."

"Tell me, then, thy doctrine, and expound to me thy hopes," said Glaucus earnestly.

Olinthus was not slow to obey that prayer; and there, as oftentimes in the early ages of the Christian creed, it was in the darkness of the dungeon, and over the approach of death, that the dawning Gospel shed its soft and consecrating rays.

It was thus that the evangel spread. If we are not doing what Andrew did, let us ask ourselves the reason why. There must be a reason why. There must be a reason. Do we no longer believe in Christ? Is a man just as well off who has never heard of Christ? Do we fear the world? Is there anything in our life that condemns us when we would bring another to Christ, to the Church, to the prayer meeting, that mocks us with the cry, "Physician, heal thyself"? These are searching questions, but they are questions which ought to be asked.

THE DESTINY OF DISCIPLES

In the last address to His disciples our Lord made it very plain that He had chosen the twelve that they might work for Him among the nations of the earth.

"Ye have not chosen Me, but I have chosen you and ordained you, that ye should go and bring forth fruit, and that your fruit should remain" (John 15:16). "These things have I spoken unto you that your joy might be full (v. 11)." Our purpose as disciples of Jesus is to bear fruit. Neither His joy nor our joy can be full unless we bear fruit. What fruit was that which the first disciples brought to the feet of Jesus! Samuel Rutherford's first church was at Anwoth on the Solway. There he wrestled, like Jacob with the Angel, with God for his few sheep in the wilderness. His letters express his yearnings for the souls that he ministered to there and his love for that first church. These are not his own words, but are built about words that he frequently employed, and they express the joy of the true minister of Christ and the privilege of every disciple of Jesus; yes, the high duty of every follower of His:

> O Anwoth by the Solway,
> To me thou still art dear,
>   E'en from the gate of Heaven
> I'll drop for thee a tear.
>   Oh, if one soul from Anwoth
> Meet me at God's right hand,
>   My heaven will be two heavens
> In Immanuel's Land.

2

PHILIP

Philip does not scintillate. He makes no great blunders, neither does he attract attention by striking deeds or brilliant sayings. To me he is the common, everyday Christian, following his Master faithfully; no son of thunder, either for good or for evil; not always seeing the reason for things as they come and go; a little dull at times in catching the meaning of the words and acts of Christ, but nevertheless continuing in His steps; an average two-talent sort of Christian, and therefore, perhaps, more than any of the Twelve a type of those who were to believe on the Name of Jesus.

Because of his Greek name and the fact that it was to him first of all that the inquiring Greeks came when they desired to see Jesus, it has been thought that Philip had Greek connections. This is possible. Or it may have been just by accident that the Greeks happened to come upon Philip first among the disciples. But, whether by choice or by accident, their first approaching Philip was a fortunate event. He was a man who would hear carefully what they had to say and take time for a decision.

I can imagine that if the Greeks had come first to the Sons of Thunder, John or James, or even Peter, they would have told them to be gone, that Jesus had nothing to say to Greeks or other Gentiles, but only to the children of Abraham. But when they say to Philip, "We would see Jesus," they come upon a man who receives them kindly and, if not making a decision himself, sees that their cause has a fair hearing.

Philip took them to Andrew, evidently counting on his sympa-

21

thy and on his sound advice, and then Philip and Andrew took the Greeks to Jesus. This first appeal from the world outside of Israel stirred our Savior to the depths of His being. In these inquiring, reverent Greeks He saw the prophecy of the great host that, out of Greece and Rome and Africa and Britain and America, would come to follow Him and believe on His Name, finding in Him the Way, the Truth and the Life. He beheld the long procession of saints and martyrs coming from the east and the west, the north and the south. What wonder that He exclaimed, "Father, glorify Thy Name!"

PHILIP THE APPROACHABLE

In Philip, then, we have a man who, in the small band of disciples, himself an Hebrew, was nevertheless an approachable man not out of touch or sympathy with the world that differed from his own world. He was not a Christian who had become "churchified" so as to lose all touch with people outside the Church, unable to meet with them or talk with them. We believe that Jesus is the only Way, Truth and Life, and we know that the light of natural religion is not enough to guide a man to salvation, else had Christ not died. Yet we like to think that always "other sheep not of this fold" belong to Christ and that in ways unknown to you and me Christ draws them unto Himself.

It was Philip who, at the Last Supper, asked one of the questions which elicited from Jesus the memorable answers. He had said, "Whither I go ye know and the way ye know." That moved Thomas to exclaim, "Lord, we know not whither Thou goest, and how can we know the way?" To this Jesus replied, "I am the Way, the Truth and the Life. No man cometh unto the Father but by Me. If ye had known Me, ye should have known My Father also." Then Philip asked the question that so often lies unspoken in our minds, that question which underlies all religion —no dull, stupid question as is so often thought, but the great fundamental question—"Lord, show us the Father and it sufficeth us!"

For years now Philip had heard Jesus speak of God as His Father, and of how He had come to do the Father's will and how He and the Father were one. Philip was perplexed by the relationship, as many a Christian since has been, and he thought he would clear the whole atmosphere by this question about God. Whatever he was or was not, Philip knew how to ask a great question. It is no common gift. Some men can teach more by questions than others can by declarations or answers. Who was this Father? Where was He? How would He appear? Show me the Father!

How often, how often, looking at night up into the starry heavens, so calm, so luminous, so glorious, we have asked ourselves, "Where is He that made them? Why does He hide Himself so wondrously as if there were no God at all?" Or, in the midst of great waters, all the billows of fate and disaster sweeping over the soul, we have asked the same question, "Lord, who art Thou that runnest upon me? Where art Thou? Why art Thou far from helping me, O my God?"

Jesus, who was made in all things like unto His brethren, uttered the same cry, passed through that same gulf of temporary yearning and uncertainty about God. "And about the ninth hour Jesus cried with a loud voice saying, Eloi, Eloi, lama sabachthani— which is, being interpreted, My God, My God, why hast Thou forsaken Me?" A God who has forsaken us is a God who is not. Yes, could we but interpret many a cry and many a prayer that is wrung from human lips, of all races, creeds and tongues, we should find, I think, that being interpreted in the universal language of the soul it means this: "Why hast Thou forsaken me? Where is God? Who is God?" To hold to our faith in God, that is where the battle of life is won or lost. "Cast me not away from Thy presence!"

JOB THE THE TEMPEST-TOSSED

Yes, with tempest-tossed Job our soul cries out, "Oh that I knew where I might find Him! That I might come even to His seat! I would order my cause before Him and fill my mouth with arguments. I would know the words which He would answer me, and understand what He would say unto me. Behold I go forward, but He is not there, and backward, but I cannot perceive Him: on the left hand where He doth work, but I cannot behold Him; He hideth Himself on the right hand that I cannot see Him." Happy are we if we can take the next note in Job's song and sing with him, "But He knoweth the way that I take, and when He hath tried me I shall come forth as gold."

JESUS IS THE ANSWER

Jesus Christ is the answer to humanity's cry. More than we think it, judging by those who resort to houses of prayer and worship, men in some way ask themselves Philip's great question about God. That man must trouble himself with such a question—that, made in God's image, he must yet wonder if there is a God and how God works and what He is—is one of the sad results of sin. Something dreadful has happened: man's natural and easy fellowship with God has been broken, broken by human sin, and thus it is that Christ, taking upon Himself our nature and bearing our sins, had, when He was dying on the Cross, that same experience of the broken fellowship; God drifted from Him. "My God, why hast Thou forsaken Me?" But He was forsaken that we might never be forsaken. Still He walks among men, into the dark house of sorrow, through the corridors of pain in the hospital, amid the debris and human wreckage of the awful battlefields where men like beasts have fought with beasts, and with infinite compassion and tenderness answers all these cries, saying, "He that hath seen Me hath seen the Father." Not "God"; that is too remote, philosophical. Jesus seldom uses the word "God." His favorite expression, full of tender meaning, was "Father." "He that hath seen Me hath seen the Father!" At the beginning of the great discourse at the Supper Table, Jesus had said, "Let not your hearts be troubled: ye believe in God, believe also in Me." But here He reverses the argument, "Ye know Me, ye have seen and heard Me, ye trust Me as your Friend and Master, ye believe in Me, believe also in God. He that hath seen Me hath seen the Father also."

With that great saying, and without discussing the relationship existing between the members of the adorable Trinity, Father, Son and Holy Spirit, let us comfort our hearts. We know that Christ has come; that Jesus lived and died and rose again; that His words are before us. Whatever this world may seem to say of God, stars, seas, wind-bowed forests, tragedies in nature and in man's life, losses, griefs, shipwrecks, hurricanes, whirlwinds of misfortune and disaster, let us remember that the final and authoritative word about God, as Father and Redeemer, is Jesus Christ.

A FINAL WORD

I end these meditations upon Philip by going back to the beginning. "The day following Jesus would go forth into Galilee, and findeth Philip, and saith unto him, Follow Me. Now Philip was of Bethsaida, the city of Andrew and Peter. Philip findeth Nathaniel, and saith unto him, We have found Him, of whom Moses in the law and the prophets did write, Jesus of Nazareth, the son of Joseph. And Nathaniel said unto him, Can there any good thing come out of Nazareth?"

Nathaniel was a very thoughtful, probably mentally trained man and philosopher. He thinks it absurd that the Messiah should be found in Nazareth. Perhaps that expression of prejudice was intended only as the introductory remarks to a long discussion about the Messias, when and where He should make His appearance. But Philip, who was no logician, no philosopher, only a plain man with a great deal of common sense, interrupted all Nathaniel's learned discussion by saying, "Come and see."

He did not get angry with Nathaniel for doubting his judgment, nor did he debate with him the matter. He simply said, "Come and see." Jesus Christ likes that test. Some men may have a reputation for wisdom or piety, but would shrink from examination on these points. Christ welcomes the test. "Come and see." It is the best reason we can give when we ask anyone to believe on Jesus. More than that, it is an invitation that oftentimes we must extend to ourselves, to our own doubting hearts or rebellious will, "Come and see."

You have been following Christ, but, like Peter, afar off. Come nearer, nearer, so that you can trace the lineaments of the Divine countenance. Come and see if He is not the Fountain of Life. Come and see if He is not able to restore and forgive. "O taste and see that the Lord is good. Blessed is the man that trusteth in Him."

3

MATTHEW THE PUBLICAN

I call Matthew, by way of description, the "publican," for that was his own account of himself. Mark and Luke, in their catalogues of the disciples, call him just Matthew, with no descriptive or qualifying words, but Matthew in his own enumeration of the Twelve (Matt. 20:3), when he comes to name himself, writes, "Matthew the publican." It has little meaning for remote ears today, but it meant a great deal for any man to be called a publican in Matthew's day, and it meant a great deal of humility, of unfeigned sorrow, yet of abounding joy, too, over his change of state and fortune, for Matthew to put himself down as a "publican."

A publican! No name was so hateful to the Jews of that day, for no office was so detested. "Publicans and sinners" was the common saying of the people then. It was equivalent, a symbol, of degradation, of loss of character and self-respect, of public scorn and contempt. It was the publican's business to collect the taxes imposed by the Roman government. He was thus a representative of the rulers and enslavers of Israel. His title was a title of infamy, for he was the underling of the wealthy Roman officers who farmed the taxes, paying so much for the privilege of collecting the taxes in a given district, and then gouging out of the people, their helpless victims, as much as they could in excess of the contract price. The burden of taxation was heavy upon the people, who had to satisfy the cupidity of their native rulers and also that of the Roman empire.

The income of Herod the Great is said to have been 1,600 talents, or $3,400,000. Any man who held this post of tax collector was bound to be hated by the people, but double was the hatred and scorn when the office was held by a member of their own race, and still worse, when that Hebrew, as in the case of Matthew, was a member of the sacred tribe of Levi.

Jesus had come to "His own city"; that is, Capernaum, His adopted home. He was in the house of Peter, or some other house, when it was noised abroad that He was there and a great crowd gathered within and without. As Jesus was preaching to them, four men brought one who was sick of the palsy, and, unable to get near Jesus for the press of the crowd, they uncovered the roof and let down the sick man before Him. When He saw their faith Jesus healed the paralytic, saying to him, "Son, thy sins be forgiven thee," and, when the Scribes and Pharisees took exception to that, "Arise, take up thy bed and walk. And immediately he arose and took up the bed and went forth before them all, inasmuch that they were all amazed, and glorified God, saying, We never saw it on this fashion" (Mark 2:11, 12).

MEET MATTHEW

Leaving the crowded house and congested highway Jesus went forth again by the seaside, and as he passed by He saw Matthew sitting at the receipt of custom and "He said unto him, 'Follow Me.' And he left all, rose up, and followed Him" (Luke 5:27, 28). I like to think that Matthew, like the other publican who came to Christ, Zacchaeus, was a rich man, and when Luke writes that "he left all" it means that Matthew forsook a lucrative, if ignoble, calling for the humble friendship of Christ. He probably had more to leave than any of the Twelve. John Keble, in *The Christian Year*, thus beautifully celebrates the call of Matthew:

> At once he rose, and left his gold;
> His treasure and his heart
>   Transferred, where he shall safe behold
> Earth and her idols part;
>   While he beside his endless store
>   Shall sit and floods unceasing pour
>   Of Christ's true riches o'er all time and space,
>   First angel of His Church, first steward of His grace!

It is significant that Mark and Luke in their account of the call of Matthew do not call him Matthew, but Levi. The supposition is that when he became a disciple of Jesus, Matthew assumed a new name, like Peter and Paul, and that his new name was to him the sign and symbol of his new life. Already Christ had given him that "new name" that He has promised to faithful believers (Rev. 2:17). Levi, the renegade Jew, the publican, the deserter, the traitor, the infamous one, was dead, and a new man, Matthew, the disciple of Jesus, had been born. As Victor Hugo wrote of Jean Valjean, now the prosperous mayor of M— sur M—, all that he had done was a hole in which he had buried his past life and his old name.

A TRANSFORMED TRAITOR

Matthew is thus to be distinguished among the Twelve as the man in whom already Christ, before the period of training, had wrought a profound transformation. Peter, Andrew, James, John, Philip and Nathaniel were all earnest, devout Jews, perhaps all of them disciples of the great reformer, John the Baptist, when they became disciples of Jesus. That new relationship, when we consider their character and the nature of John's teaching, was a natural step in advance for them; it indicated spiritual growth rather than moral transformation and spiritual revolution. But with Matthew it was different: he was, at least in public estimation, a sinner, an abandoned creature, a man past saving or helping, a traitor to all good things, the last man in the world to be interested in John or in Jesus. For him to leave the lucrative business of the tax collector and join himself to the wandering disciples of Jesus meant a profound moral change, a mighty upheaval in his soul. For this reason Matthew in his very call was a type of the moral transformation which Christ is able to effect in men's lives. By calling Matthew to follow him, Jesus showed that He was able to save even to the uttermost all who come unto Him.

It took courage for Matthew to follow Christ, for this renegade Hebrew, this apostate Levite, this tool of the despised tax lords to enter into the fellowship of men like Peter and James and John. But whatever the price was, Matthew paid it gladly. He succeeded not only in winning the confidence and friendship of the zealous Jews who were now his companions, but he lived to write the great Gospel in which he makes honorable amends for his erst-while apostasy by showing how Jesus is the fulfiller of Old Testament prophecy, quoting the Old Testament sixty-five times and calling Jesus the Son of David eight times. Remember, when you are reading this Gospel, this most Hebrew of all the four, that it was written by Matthew, the faithful disciple of Jesus, but once Levi the son of Alphaeus, the publican and apostate, the man who had sold his Levitical birthright for a mess of Roman pottage.

A Famous Feast

The only other incident in which Matthew figures in the Gospel narratives is that of the feast which he made for Jesus, the "great feast," as Luke terms it. Matthew modestly says that Jesus was sitting at meat in "the" house, but Mark and Luke tell us that the house was Matthew's (Mark 2:15; Luke 5:29). He meant it as an honor to his new Master, perhaps also as a sort of farewell to his old friends and associates, for "there was a great company of publicans and sinners and others" (Mark and Luke). It is possible to overdo the appeal of Christ to the poor and humble. He speaks to other classes as well, and here we have Him entertained at a costly banquet by His well-to-do disciple, Matthew. That was Matthew's natural way of showing respect to Jesus. He knew how to entertain, how to have a supper, a feast, and he made Jesus such an offering. The presence of Jesus among the publicans scandalized the Scribes and Pharisees, who said to the disciples of Jesus, "How is it that He eateth and drinketh with publicans and sinners?" (Mark 2:16). Their exception gave Jesus opportunity for one of His most telling sentence sermons. Accepting satirically, of course, their estimate of themselves as righteous and of the publicans as sinners, He said, "They that are whole have no need of the physician, but they that are sick: I came not to call the righteous, but sinners to repentance." It was an overwhelming bit of irony. Then he changed His tone and said, "Go ye and learn what that meaneth, I will have mercy and not sacrifice," thereby implying that what the Pharisees and Scribes called righteousness was not acceptable to God.

Jesus could eat and drink with publicans and sinners. Sometimes the Christian minister or worker, especially the Christian minister, feels that he is circumscribed by custom and convention in his efforts for Christ. The crowded saloon, the haunts of loose women and fast men, afford a rich field for labor. But did he go into these places, he fears that he would not come out with as much honor as Jesus did. Many an overzealous minister has ruined his reputation and hurt, rather than helped, the cause of Christ by indiscretions in this respect. I remember a prominent minister who, in order to secure evidence that liquor was being sold in disorderly houses in one of our great cities, himself made a round of investigation in the guise of a patron of those places. He suffered the inevitable consequences of such unthinkable folly. The servant of Christ, harmless as the dove, must also be wise as the serpent.

A CONSERVATIVE CHRISTIAN

Matthew, finally, is a type of the conservative Christian. He put great value on the past. The great effort of his Gospel is to show that the life and ministry of Christ fulfilled the Scriptures and the prophecies. He does not begin to talk about Christ, about God, about religion in that tone which has become so popular in our day, as if the writer or speaker were the "first that ever burst" upon the silent sea of faith, as if he were a pioneer in religious thought and endeavor. The magnificent past, the words that God at sundry times and in divers manners spake in times past unto the Fathers, Matthew did not scorn, but treasured, and over them he pondered. He was not the man who would try to put a fool's cap upon all the past religious history of man, but made it a foundation upon which to stand, a giant's shoulder, as it were, from which he might look farther into the future and into the mysteries of God than those who stood merely upon the ground of their own experience.

Christianity assumes magnificent proportions when we take it with its splendid Old Testament background. It becomes a sublime plan, an unfolding panorama of God's power and grace, "even the mystery which hath been hid from ages and from generations, but now is made manifest to the saints, to whom God would make known what is the riches of the glory of this mystery among the Gentiles; which is Christ in you, the hope of glory" (Col. 1:26, 27).

Like all grand things prophecy has been fearfully abused, defamed by charlatans whose expositions are mere impositions. But that abuse ought not to turn the Church from this great field of assurance and of hope. Indeed, the distinctive thing about the evidence of Christianity on the apologetic side is its prophetic element. The fine mind of Pascal has expressed as none other could this argument:

> The greatest of the proofs of Jesus Christ are the prophecies. They are also what God has the most provided for; for the event which has fulfilled them is a miracle which has subsisted from the birth of the Church even to the end. During sixteen hundred years, therefore, God raised up a succession of prophets; and, in the four hundred years that succeeded, He dispersed all these prophecies, with the Jews who bore them, into all parts of the world. This, then, was the preparation for the birth of Jesus Christ, whose Gospel was to be believed by the whole world, it was necessary, not only that there should be prophecies, to make Him be believed, but that these prophecies should be everywhere in the world, in order to cause Him to be embraced by the whole world.
>
> Prophecies—even if one man had made a book of predictions of Jesus Christ, both of the time and the manner of His coming, and if Jesus Christ had come in conformity with these prophecies, this would be of infinite weight. But there is much more here. There is a succession of men, who come, during four thousand years, constantly and without variation, one after another, predicting the same event. A whole people announce Him, and subsist during four thousand years in order to render as a body testimony of the assurances which they have of Him and from which they can be turned by no menaces and persecutions: this is much more important.

Such a man was Matthew. If we read his Gospel, we will meet the man—in its pages and between its lines.

4

SIMON THE ZEALOT

I take up the study of the disciple called Simon Zelotes immediately after that of Matthew the publican for the reason that they present such a contrast, and in their persons illustrate the catholicity of Jesus and the universality of His Church. Worldly prudence would have forbidden the selection of both Matthew and Simon—of Matthew because he was a hated publican, a renegade Jew and an apostate Levite; of Simon because he erred on the other side, being a Zealot, that is, a member of the extreme revolutionary and radical party. The utmost concession that worldly prudence would have made would be to sanction the selection of one of these men, but not of both of them. Bad enough to have either type in a band of men that was to establish the spiritual throne of Israel, but still worse to have them both together in the same fellowship. But Jesus showed at the very beginning that His kingdom was not of this world. None would have chosen as He chose; none would have built as He commenced to build. He took a detested publican and a fiery agitator into the same company of his disciples. The tax collector and the tax hater both followed Jesus.

In his article on Matthew Dr. John Kitto writes, "Few things are more suggestive to the thoughtful mind than the scantiness of our knowledge of the lives and actions of the apostles and evangelists of our Lord. Of several of the Twelve nothing beyond the names has reached us; others are barely mentioned in the Gospel narrative, and that chiefly in the way of blame or remonstrance.

Of the very chiefest of them, the thing to be noted is not what we know but what we do not know. Of their work in the evangelism of the world little or nothing remains beyond vague traditions."

A REBEL WITH A CAUSE

We feel this scantiness of material when we come to speak of Simon, for we know nothing of him save that he was one of the Twelve and that he was called the Zealot, also the Canaanite—both names have a party significance. It is only his epithet that justifies us in venturing to speak of Simon. Most scholars agree that this epithet, "the Zealot," "connects Simon unmistakably with the famous party which rose in rebellion under Judas in the days of the taxing, some thirty years before Christ's ministry began, when Judaea and Samaria were brought under the direct government of Rome, and the census of the population was taken with a view to subsequent taxation." Gamaliel's speech before the council advising moderation in dealing with Peter and John, as recorded in Acts the fifth chapter, gives us the history of that insurrection: "Ye men of Israel, take heed to yourselves what ye intend to do as touching these men. For before these days rose up Theudas, boasting himself to be somebody; to whom a number of men, about four hundred, joined themselves: who was slain; and all, as many as obeyed him, were scattered and brought to naught. After this man rose up Judas of Galilee, in the days of the taxing, and drew away much people after him: he also perished; and all, even as many as obeyed him, were dispersed."

The fires of this insurrection still smouldered in the days of Jesus' ministry, and it is reasonable to think that Simon belonged to this party, a Hebrew revolutionary. If the contrast between Simon and Matthew was great, still greater the contrast between Simon and Jesus. "How singular a phenomenon," writes Alexander Bruce, "is this ex-zealot among the disciples of Jesus. No two men could differ more widely in their spirit, ends and means than Judas of Galilee and Jesus of Nazareth. The one was a political malcontent; the other would have the conquered bow to the yoke and give to Caesar Caesar's due. The former aimed at restoring the kingdom of Israel, adopting for his watchword 'We have no Lord or Master but God'; the latter aimed at founding a kingdom, not national, but universal; not of this world, but purely spiritual. The means employed by the two actors were as diverse as their ends. One had recourse to the carnal weapons of war, the sword and the dagger; the other relied solely on the gentle but omnipotent force of truth." (*The Training of the Twelve*, page 34.)

A NEW MAN

I do not think that the fiery enthusiasm of Simon was permitted to burn itself out, but that now it burned to a better end, burned with devotion to Christ and to His universal empire. Like Peter, like John, like Paul, Simon, when he became a disciple of Jesus, was the same personality, the same character, but with a new aim and a new object for his powers. It is true that the Church has suffered and does now suffer from the efforts of those who have zeal, but not according to knowledge. The successive waves of lay movements within the Church in recent years which have rolled up the beach with much noise and fury and suddenly subsided might be instanced as zeal, but not according to knowledge. But if the Church has suffered from that kind of zeal, still more has it suffered from the lack of any kind of zeal. How many of us have any qualifications for repeating the words of the Psalmist which Jesus applied to Himself, "The zeal of Thine house hath eaten me up"?

> Holy Spirit, Truth Divine,
> Dawn upon this soul of mine;
> > Word of God, and inward Light,
> Wake my spirit, clear my sight.

> Holy Spirit, Love Divine,
> Glow within this heart of mine;
> > Kindle every high desire;
> Perish self in Thy pure fire!

The zeal of Simon poured itself forth in the form of patriotism. By a thrust of the sword, had it been possible, he would have restored the Kingdom of Israel. When he became an apostle his energies were directed towards the establishment of a greater kingdom. How long it was before Simon came to an understanding of what the kingdom meant we do not know. But we do know that at the very last His disciples asked Jesus, "Wilt Thou at this time restore again the kingdom to Israel?" (Acts 1:6). Only the fires of Pentecost and the educative and expanding influences of their subsequent ministry let them know what Christ meant by the restoration of His kingdom and its unworldly nature. But ideally, at least, the apostle and disciple of Jesus is a man who prays and strives for the coming of the kingdom of God.

A Christian Patriot

Simon is transformed from the Hebrew patriot to the Christian patriot. The change that was wrought in Him is one that is not easily accomplished. It was the work of the Holy Spirit. The transformation remains the great need of the Church, of the Christian disciple, that he should become in regard to his faith denationalized and rise to the true dignity and responsibility of his citizenship in the kingdom—or better, commonwealth—which is heaven.

The failure of the nations as a whole to take seriously Christ's teachings about the universality of His kingdom, and the putting, when it came to the test, of the claims of the nation above the claims of Christ has been responsible for much of the riot and bloodshed and misery of mankind. The unknown author of the *Epistle to Diognetus*, describing the Christians of his age, true at least of some of them, thus powerfully outlines true Christianity in the world:

> The Christians, he says, are not distinguished from other men by country, language, nor by civil institutions. For they neither dwell in cities by themselves, nor use a peculiar tongue, nor lead a singular mode of life. They dwell in the Grecian or barbarian cities, as the cities may be; they follow the usage of the country in dress, food and the other affairs of life. Yet they present a wonderful and confessedly paradoxical conduct. They dwell in their own native lands, but as strangers. They take part in all things, as citizens; and they suffer all things, as foreigners. Every foreign country is a fatherland to them, and every native land is a foreign.
>
> By the Jews they are attacked as aliens, and by the Greeks persecuted; and the cause of the enmity their enemies cannot tell. In short, what the soul is in the body, the Christians are in the

world. The soul is diffused through all the members of the body, and the Christians are spread through the cities of the world. The soul dwells in the body, but it is not of the body; so the Christians dwell in the world, but are not of the world.

How, save in the sense of irony, could this be said of the mass of Christians today? Higher than ever have risen the fierce tides of nationalism, and further and further away seems the mirage of Christianity, men living and dwelling together on the face of the earth as men whose commonwealth is grander than the Roman, or the Hebrew, or the British, or the American. We like to feel that this ideal, however stony the soil in which Christ sowed, has fallen on ground not altogether barren and has not been without fruit. I believe that in America, in Germany, in France, in England, in Russia there are devout souls not a few who not only name the Name of Christ and are familiar with His work of redemption, but who also are familiar with the ideal of a worldwide kingdom of faith, superseding all other kingdoms, in which there shall be neither Greek nor Roman, bond nor free, German nor French, American nor Russian, but all one in Christ's Name and in His Spirit.

THE COMING COMMONWEALTH

The true Christian must salute that day. He must salute the day when all national anthems shall blend into one great chorus of the nations, people of every tribe and kindred and people and tongue, ascribing majesty and glory to the Lamb slain from the foundation of the world. We hail the day when they shall bring the honor and the glory of the nations into the city of our God. It is only when the Christian commonwealth thus outranks the world's commonwealths, so dear to our world-loving hearts, that it will be possible, or advisable, to beat the sword into the ploughshare or the spear into the pruning-hook.

On a late moonlight walk through the country one summer I came to the turning of the road where a lane branched off into the forest. Immediately that lane, losing itself among the shadows of the trees, brought before me that ideal of a universal kingdom of faith. Why? Because at the end of that lane stood a somewhat dilapidated farmhouse where an old veteran of the Civil War had lived with his three sons. One of them I had remembered as a sophomore at college, how he concluded his oration with quoting Tennyson's lines in *Locksley Hall*,

> Till the war drum throbs no longer
>   And the battle flags are furled
> In the Parliament of Man,
>   The Federation of a World.

Not long after the delivery of that stirring oration he disappeared, a star, as it were, extinguished in blackness of darkness forever, his great talent lost in a terrible adventure of fleshly passion, forever dropped out of view of his friends and contemporaries. But still his eloquent quotation kept sounding in my ears as I paused to look down the lane and thought of the tragic conclusion of what had promised to be a notable career. I thought, too, on that lovely moonlight night—the graceful branches of the trees holding out their leaves as a lace work for the golden harvest moon to shine through, the kine and the horses grazing peacefully in the nearby fields, the light gleaming from the window of a distant farmhouse of Christ's plan for the world. Will it ever be realized? Will the day ever come when patriotism for His state, His kingdom will shake men with the mighty enthusiasm which they now experience as they go forth to make war against the enemies of their country? "Even so come, Lord Jesus!"

5

JAMES THE LESS

The question of the identity of this James, whether or not he is James the brother of the Lord, the pillar of the Church and the author of the epistle bearing the name of James, is declared by Dr. Neander to be the most difficult in apostolic history. The discussion of critical questions does not fall within the scope of these studies, but I shall state the reasons that have been adduced for thinking that James the Less and James the brother of the Lord are one and the same person.

In the four catalogues of the Twelve as given in Matthew, Mark, Luke and the Acts, this second James is called the son of Alphaeus, Mark in his account of the crucifixion calling him James the Less, or "little," either because of his low stature or because he was younger than James, the son of Zebedee. The chief reason for identifying James the Less with James the brother of the Lord is the reference in Paul's letter to the Galatians, where Paul tells of his visit to Jerusalem and his fifteen days with Peter, and then adds, "But other of the apostles saw I none, save James the Lord's brother" (Gal. 1:19). But the Gospels tell us of just two apostles of Christ who bore the name of James; one of these was the brother of John and the son of Zebedee, the other was the son of Alphaeus. But at once the objection will be made: how could James the son of Alphaeus be the same as James the brother of the Lord? One was the son of Alphaeus, the other the son of Joseph. The way out of this difficulty has been found by making James, together with Joses, Simon and Judas (not Iscariot) the cousins of Jesus, and called "brethren," not in the sense of uterine brothers, but kinsfolk or blood relationship, a not unheard-of usage.

This would mean that Mary, the mother of Jesus, and Mary, the mother of James, who is mentioned among those present at the cross (Mark 15:40; Matt. 27:56) were sisters. John says, "There stood by the cross of Jesus His mother, and His mother's sister, Mary, the wife of Cleophas, and Mary Magdalene" (John 19:25). If the words "His mother's sister" are to be taken in apposition with those immediately following, "Mary, the wife of Cleophas," then the meaning is that Mary, the mother of Jesus, had a sister, also called Mary, and that she was the wife of Alphaeus. Alphaeus is another form of the name Cleophas. Thus, James would be the son of Mary, the sister of the mother of Jesus, the wife of Cleophas, also called Alphaeus, and, therefore, the cousin of Jesus. In Matthew 13:55 we read, "Is not this the carpenter's son? is not His mother called Mary? and His brethren, James, and Joses, and Simon, and Judas?" And Matthew in his account of the crucifixion (Matt. 27:56) mentions among these present at the cross, "Mary, the mother of James and Joses."

WHICH JAMES WAS HE?

If these four men, James, Joses, Simon and Judas, are the cousins, or in looser terminology, the brothers of Jesus, then only one of them, Joses, is not included in the number of the Twelve. But if all but one of the brethren of Christ were among His chosen Apostles, how can this be reconciled with the statement that his own brethren did not believe on Him (John 7:5)? The usual answer is that John merely meant to say that their faith was wavering, imperfect, that they did not believe as they should, as they one day would believe on Him. In the Acts, Luke says that in addition to the eleven disciples there were together praying in the upper chamber "the women, and Mary the mother of Jesus, . . . and His brethren" (Acts 1:14). This testimony about the brethren would seem to solve, at least considerably reduce, the difficulty about His brothers not believing on Him, but, on the other hand, since James the son of Alphaeus is mentioned as one of the eleven apostles present, the addendum "and with His brethren" looks as if the writer did not consider any of the eleven apostles as brethren of Christ. Indeed, there are very good reasons for identifying the son of Alphaeus with the brother of the Lord, and also very good reasons for taking them as distinct, different individuals.

A ROLE TO FILL

One might take the epithet applied to James, "the less," and speak of the necessary part to be played by the undistinguished disciple. James, the Son of Thunder, was needed by Christ, but so was James the Less, the comparatively insignificant, whose sole history is in his name. If this James is not the brother of the Lord, then we know nothing of him, as to his own characteristics, where he preached and how he witnessed. But from the testimony of Christ, we know that he kept the Word of God that Christ had committed unto them. Luke tells us that the son of Alphaeus was with the apostolic band after the ascension, and we doubt not that he remained faithful to the end and did well his part in the building up of the walls of the Christian edifice.

Traveling much through the country one summer, I was impressed with the lasting service that had been rendered by the men of past generations who built the stone bridges over the creeks and rivers, well-rounded stone arches which still bear the burdens of traffic. They were gone, all these building hands, but their works remain. Who they were none knows; what they did, what they wrought, all know. So thought Thomas Carlyle, looking one day over the bridge at Auldgarth: "A noble craft it is, that of a mason; a good building will last longer than most books, than one book in a million. The Auldgarth Bridge still spans the water silently, defies its chafing. There hangs it and will hang, grim and strong, when of all the cunning hands that piled it together, perhaps the last is now powerless in the sleep of death. O Time! O Time! wondrous and fearful art thou, yet there is in man what is above thee!"

Here, too, were leafy avenues of oak or elm or locust trees. The hands that planted the trees could hardly have profited by them, for the planters had gone to their graves by the white churches on the hilltops before the trees had come to maturity. It was a noble service rendered to the future, to the next generation. God makes use of man's own plans and ambitions and thereby man will unconsciously serve the tomorrow of humanity. But the highest form of human greatness has always seemed to me that effort which a man puts forth in his generation, knowing that he cannot profit by it, but that generations to come will profit. Of such is the race of tree-planters. They sleep in unknown or unheeded graves, but the trees that they planted give shade to man and shelter to the birds of the air.

A veteran of the Civil War said to me several years ago, speaking of the world conflict then raging, "Everybody wants to be an officer in this war!" The indictment was too sweeping—not "everybody" by any means. But what he meant to say was that it struck him there were a great many of our young men who were thinking about the war more in terms of rank, of the grade they might hold or attain to, than of the great service they might render to humanity. I once heard the relatives of a New England man bitterly assailing the government because he had not been appointed to the rank for which they thought him fitted. The fact that a great cause was being served and that, after all, the service of a private in the ranks, giving his life if need be, was, in such a cause, all that a noble soul could ask— that seemed entirely to have escaped them. But the casualty lists told the tale. The private soldier won the crown of glory in the Great War, as in that other conflict of liberty sixty years ago.

In that ancient battle against the Amalekites, when David smote them in revenge for the sack of Ziklag, the three hundred men who were told off to abide by the stuff, to guard the camp, shared equally in the spoils of battle with the others whose swords were red with the blood of the invaders. "As his part is that goeth down to the battle, so shall his part be that tarrieth by the stuff: they shall part alike" (1 Sam. 30:24). That old law of David was a reflection of the Divine Law. God needs James the Son of Thunder, James the first martyr among the Twelve, but He needs as well James the Less, concerning whom no fact, save his name and his apostolic rank, has been preserved in the files of history. "They also serve who only stand and wait."

SOME CLOSING THOUGHTS

I am not convinced that this James was not the brother of the Lord, and one reason for thinking that he was is the remarkable number of similes and metaphors drawn from nature which appear in the Epistle of James and which bear a marked resemblance to those which were employed by Jesus in His teaching. A brother of the Lord would be familiar with that teaching. But if he is not, and if we know nothing of James but his name and those of his father and mother, and regardless of whether the epithet "the Less" refers only to stature or years and not to importance— still in his history and service as an apostle of the Lord Jesus Christ we have an example of a pure and altogether disinterested service for Christ. That is what will make good workmen of us all, to be impressed with the majesty of Jesus, the supremacy of the Kingdom of God, and the eternal worthwhileness of contributing our share to the advancement of that Kingdom.

The gleaming stones of the cemeteries on the hilltops, the abounding instances of shattered plans and baffled ambitions, the unsatisfactoriness of that which man has at length secured after long struggle, the poor relics of men who dreamed and toiled and wrought all about us—all this would be of a nature to cast a shadow over life and make man seriously ask himself the question, "Is it worth while?" The Apostle Paul knew that the disciples at Corinth, living in a world of vicissitude and change, perplexed and troubled, their society preyed upon by death not less remorselessly than the society of the Christless, could not help asking themselves that old question about the use of trying to live as followers of Christ, of laboring and suffering for Him. His answer for them came with a mighty reassurance at the end of the sublime argument for immortality in the first letter to the Corinthians: "Therefore, my beloved brethren, be ye steadfast, unmovable, always abounding in the work of the Lord, forasmuch as ye know that your labor is not in vain in the Lord." That is the Christian's ground and hope. Because of Christ, because of the light He has poured into life, because of the greatness of the Kingdom which He represents, they who live and toil in faith in Him cannot live and cannot toil in vain. Our labor is not in vain in the Lord. Yes, that is our goal, to labor, to stand by the truth in Christ, to be loyal to the Church, to the pastor, to God's work, to Christian service. It is the work that "pays," if I may borrow a phrase from the market place. It pays in time, and in ways beyond our thinking and our dreaming, it will pay in eternity.

Such a faithful follower was "James the Less." We may not be certain as to his exact identity. We can be sure of his commitment to follow the Savior.

6

JUDAS THE THRICE-NAMED

In Matthew he is called "Lebbaeus, whose surname is Thaddaeus," in Mark, Thaddaeus, in Acts and in Luke, "Judas of James." Hence he has been called the thrice-named disciple. Our Authorized Version fills in the ellipsis of the Greek text in Luke and Acts, which reads "Judas of James" or "James Judas," by supplying the word "brother." Then Judas is the brother of James the son of Alphaeus, a kinsman of Jesus, loosely called brother, and possibly the author of the Epistle of James.

All that we know of this disciple is the question he asked Jesus at the Last Supper, one of the four memorable questions that were put to Christ that night "Lord, how is it that You will manifest Yourself to us, and not to the world?" (John 14:22 NKJV). Jesus was trying to comfort His disciples against His death and separation from them. "I will not leave you comfortless: I will come to you. Yet a little while and the world seeth Me no more, but ye see Me: because I live ye shall live also. He that hath My commandments and keepeth them, he it is that loveth Me; and he that hath loved Me shall be loved of My Father, and I will love him and will manifest Myself to him" (John 14:18-21). This puzzled Judas as it must have puzzled all the other disciples. How could Christ appear to His disciples and yet not be seen of others, and even if He could do this, why would He desire to show Himself unto the disciples and not unto the world at large? "Lord, how is it that Thou wilt manifest Thyself unto us, and not unto the world?" (v. 22).

After the resurrection, Jesus revealed Himself to His disciples, to many who believed on His Name, but not unto the public at large. Is this what Jesus meant when He said that the world would not see Him but His disciples would see Him? Probably not. Our Lord seems to speak of His spiritual manifestation, not a corporeal one. When He gave them His final commission, He said, "Lo, I am with you always, even unto the end of the world." There, certainly, He did not mean a corporeal manifestation and presence.

The mistake of Judas had been a very common one among the disciples of Jesus and persists to this day, taking the particular form of emphasis on millennialism and the bodily advent of Christ upon the earth, not that such an appearance will not take place, but that Christ in the farewell address seeks to comfort the hearts of the disciples by assuring them of His presence with them, manifesting Himself to them in a real and most precious way, so that His disciples should take courage and comfort in Him, although the world saw nothing and believed nothing. Paul, speaking of his trial at Rome and how his friends forsook him as the disciples had once forsaken their Lord, said, "But the Lord stood with me, and strengthened me; that by me the preaching might be fully known. And the Lord shall deliver me from every evil work, and will preserve me unto His heavenly kingdom" (2 Tim. 4:17,18). Paul knew that Christ was there, manifesting Himself as his helper and friend, though Nero and the soldiers and hangers-on about the court saw nothing and felt nothing.

CHRIST'S PERENNIAL PRESENCE

Great spiritual truth lies wrapped in the somewhat obscure promises about the return of our Lord to this earth in glory and in judgment. But whatever that may be, however we try to get a mental picture of it, there is this other return and presence of Christ, not the Second Advent, but the perennial advent to those who live in Him. We do not need to wait for rending heavens and opening graves and uncovered seas to behold Christ. Even now the eye of faith may perceive Him. "Behold, I stand at the door and knock: if any man hear My voice and open the door, I will come in to him, and will sup with him, and he with Me" (Rev. 3:20).

You may have talked with Christians who have passed through great trial as by fire and who will reverently relate how the Lord Himself stood by them. There was granted unto them a blessed, mighty demonstration of His help and His companionship, an experience which will never fade from their minds. Happy are they who may have had such experience. But, surely, without claiming such overwhelming demonstration of the presence of Christ, there have been times when you saw the Lord and were helped, you looked unto Him and were not confounded. It may have been as you sat in the church and heard the accents of a hymn of grace that touched your spirit as with an angel's wand; or when your whole being cried a fervent Amen to the declaration of God's saving goodness; or in some sacramental hour of sorrow, or of joy; or at someone's death, when the Twenty-third Psalm became a great reality—"Yea, though I walk through the valley of the shadow of death, I will fear no evil, for Thou art with me"—or at someone's birth, when the glory and spirituality of life came like a flood upon your soul, and the eternal Son of God stood, as it were, before you, the Redeemer and the Benefactor of your life.

> Jesus, these eyes have never seen
> That glorious form of Thine;
> The veil of sense hangs dark between
> Thy blessed face and mine.
>
> I see Thee not, I hear Thee not,
> Yet art Thou oft with me;
> And earth hath ne'er so dear a spot
> As where I meet with Thee.
>
> Like some bright dream that comes unsought,
> When slumbers o'er me roll,
> Thine image ever fills my thought,
> And charms my ravished soul.

Yes, the disciples may see Christ when the world does not. The great temptation of Christian disciples today is to be dismayed and frightened when they learn that the world cannot or will not see Him whom the believer sees. Hence, the half-sad, half-humorous efforts that are made to destroy the supernatural element in the

Christian religion, to try and accommodate Christianity to the doubts and skepticism and even to the infidelity of the world. But did Christ ever say that His Church and the world would see eye to eye? Did He tell His disciples that they were to be disturbed when the world did not believe as they believed? Far from it. He told them plainly of the world's dissent, of the world's enmity, of the world's complete inability to see Him, to realize His presence. If your Christian faith is not strong enough to keep you from fear when you find that others deny, even ridicule, all that you have received and believed, your own belief, your own hopes, your own love for Christ and faith in God and hope of forgiveness through His blood and of the life that is to come—they are but poor things indeed, mere reeds shaken with the wind.

JESUS ANSWERS JUDAS

The answer of Jesus to the question of Judas, it is to be observed, ignores the thing that troubled Judas, a manifestation to the Twelve but not to the world. Perhaps, at that stage Judas and the others could not receive it (John 16:25). What He does explain in His great answer is the condition upon which a disciple of Christ receives the Divine manifestation and knows in his heart of hearts that Christ is and that He ever lives to help him and uphold him. That condition is grand in its simplicity—obedience: "If a man love Me, Judas, he will keep My words: and My Father will love him, and we will come unto him, and make our abode with him" (John 14:23). It is the old law that moral fidelity is the law of spiritual illumination, that if one does what is right he will come to know what is true. How many times and with what divers tones the Word of God declares this truth which Christ stated to Judas! "Unto the upright there ariseth light in the darkness" (Psalm 112:4); "Light is sown for the righteous, and gladness for the upright in heart" (Psalm 97:11); "The secret of the Lord is with them that fear Him" (Psal'n 25:14); "The path of the just is as the shining light, that shineth more and more unto the perfect day" (Prov. 4:18); "Blessed are the pure in heart; for they shall see God" (Matt. 5:8).

We feel at times the shadowy ways, the vagueness of all our faith. But what of this old law of obedience, of love for God, of keeping the words of Jesus? Holy Spirit, Illuminator of my conscience, let Your light shine upon my path! Where You point, let me go, when You call let me obey. Let me be true to the light that I have, and You will grant me more light, and I shall know if I follow on to know the Lord. I know, I confess, that in the past I have forfeited joy, I have missed seeing my Savior, I have lost opportunity for doing good, because I have not kept His words, because I have not been faithful to the light that was given me. Forgive me, O Holy Spirit of truth, You who make Christ and God real to us, for past offenses and past disobedience, and let me know the joy and peace of those who see their Lord and cry, "My Lord and my God!" because they have done His will, have kept His words!

7

BARTHOLOMEW

Of all the apostles of whose call to follow Jesus there is left us a record in the Gospels, Bartholomew was the only one who hesitated. All the others rose up at once and followed. Bartholomew was not convinced when the first invitation came to him through Philip, and even when he met Jesus he had some questions to ask Him before he became His disciple (John 1:46-49). But, just as Thomas doubted concerning the resurrection of Christ only to come at length to a belief in it which expressed itself in the greatest confession in Christian history, so Bartholomew hesitated at first about becoming the disciple of Jesus but ended by hailing Him as the Son of God.

From the foregoing it will be seen that I identify Nathaniel with Bartholomew. It cannot be proven that they are one and the same person.

ONE AND THE SAME?

The reason for so thinking is the fact that Matthew, Mark and Luke in their enumeration of the Twelve speak of a Bartholomew but not of a Nathanael, whereas John tells of Nathaniel but knows nothing of Bartholomew. John relates how Philip brought Nathaniel to Jesus, and in the lists of the Twelve in the other three Gospels Philip and Nathaniel are always mentioned together. It is thus altogether probable that the Nathaniel of John is the Bartholomew of Matthew, Mark and Luke—Nathaniel being his chief name and Bartholomew indicating his filial relationship, meaning son of Tolmai.

The finest natures sometimes surprise us with their bondage of prejudice. On all other subjects fair and generous, there will be one subject upon which they are unreasonable and the children of prejudice. Bartholomew was not a slave to prejudice, but he was subject to its influence, for when Philip sought him out and said to him, "We have found Him of whom Moses in the law, and the prophets did write, Jesus of Nazareth, the son of Joseph"; Bartholomew answered, "Can there any good thing come out of Nazareth?" The reply has become proverbial, expressing one's disbelief in noble or distinguished qualities in certain persons or worthy characters from certain places.

HUMILITY OR PRIDE?

As Bartholomew was himself a Galilean, perhaps it was not so much from pride and scorn, as might have been the case with a Judean, that he raised this question about Nazareth, as from an unworthy humility. He had come to share in the sentiments entertained beyond the borders of his province that nothing good nor great could ever come out of Galilee, especially that little town of Nazareth, and least of all the Messiah of Israel. But the fine thing about Bartholomew is that he did not allow this skepticism, or prejudice, whichever you like to call it, to interfere with him listening to the proof that Philip had to offer for his affirmation that he had found the Messiah.

And what was that proof? Only this: "Come and see." Christianity has nothing to hide. It has no doctrines that must be kept in the background. It would win no disciples under false pretense of being something that it is not. Jesus reveals Himself to men. He says, with Philip, "Come and see." The prejudice which exists in the mind of humanity towards the Gospel and the Savior of the Gospel, an indubitable prejudice, is an indirect tribute to its truth and its merit. The Gospel declares itself to be a message of good tidings, all that is good for man, but it also declares that the heart of man is enmity against God, that man has prejudices against his best friend. And not all who are prejudiced against the Gospel have the candor of this hesitating disciple who came and saw and believed. In the words of Dr. Robert Ellis Thompson, in his admirable sketch of the Apostles, "If men will come and see what the Gospel of the Son of God has done and is doing for our race, see the miracles of transformation it has wrought upon men's characters, see the slow and steady gains of its humanizing influences upon social ideals and usages, see the sustaining hopes and comforts it brings to the suffering, the poor and the helpless—there would be fewer sceptics in the world."

Still Jesus can appeal to His works: "Or else believe Me for the very works' sake." In answer to the laconic reply of Philip, Bartholomew went with him to see Jesus. Jesus, seeing him coming, exclaimed, "Behold an Israelite indeed, in whom there is no guile!" This is another saying from this celebrated account of the call of Bartholomew that has passed into the proverbial speech of our day, making the name of Bartholomew a synonym for sincerity. Jesus had in this disciple a solid foundation upon which to build. Sincerity is the cornerstone of character. We recognize its fundamental worth and importance because that is always the question that men ask of other men, especially those who speak or act in the Name of God, as religious workers and teachers, in the name of humanity, as philanthropic workers, or in the name of liberty and justice, as politicians and statesmen. Is the man sincere, straightforward, honest with himself and with other men? If so, we can put up with many faults and shortcomings. But if he is not, then no matter what his gifts may be, we cannot give him our admiration. The lack of sincerity will ruin any life, great or small. "With an upright man Thou wilt show Thyself upright . . . and with the froward Thou wilt show Thyself froward" (Psalm 18:25,26).

UNDER THE FIG TREE

This guileless, open-hearted, open-minded Bartholomew was astonished that Jesus would presume to pass judgment upon his character whom He had never known, possibly had never seen him, before. "Whence knowest Thou me?" Jesus answered, "Before that Philip called thee, when thou wast under the fig tree, I saw thee." Then Bartholomew said, "Rabbi, Thou art the Son of God, Thou art the King of Israel."

At first reading, this looks as if Bartholomew was amazed that

Jesus had the power to read a man's mind and that by preternatural knowledge He knew that he had been sitting under a fig tree. If this is all, then Bartholomew believes that Jesus is the Son of God simply because He possesses a strange power of telepathy and vision. But I think that there is far more here than that. It was not that Jesus knew his physical location, sitting under a fig tree, but that He knew his spiritual location, knew all that was in his heart as he sat musing and praying beneath the fig tree, understood all the pure aspirations of his heart. It was this which made Bartholomew feel that he had to deal with no ordinary person, even that the Son of God stood in the flesh before him. It was a case of "deep calling unto deep."

That is the strange, spiritual power of Jesus Christ, that He needs not that man should testify of man, or that man should testify of himself, for He knows what is in man. Bartholomew perceived how Jesus knew all the hopes and longings of his heart, the holy aspirations of his meditations, without his telling Him, and he cried out, "Thou art the Son of God!" The woman of Samaria heard Jesus tell her how many husbands she had had and the state in which she was then living, and, awed and impressed, said, "Sir, I perceive that Thou art a prophet." The great truth envisaged in the conversion of Bartholomew is that Christ is the soul's true Mate, true Companion.

Test this by your own hearts beneath the fig tree. There have been hours when the blessed mood hinted at by Wordsworth has come upon you; when mist and cloud seemed to have been swept aside, and you realized to the full your spiritual nature, your spiritual inheritance:

> That blessed mood,
> In which the burthen of the mystery,
> In which the heavy and the weary weight
> Of all this unintelligible world
> Is lightened: that serene and blessed mood,
> In which the affections gently lead us on,
> Until, the breath of this corporeal frame
> And even the motion of our human blood
> Almost suspended, we are laid asleep
> In body, and become a living soul:

> While with an eye made quiet by the power
> Of harmony and the deep power of joy,
> We see into the life of things.

The fears of life no longer haunted you; the cares of life no more harassed you; the vain strivings of life were stilled. The soul looked duty and destiny straight in the eye and did not flinch. A hunger and thirst after righteousness, a desire to be without sin or guile, a mighty yearning for whatsoever things that are high and holy and pure and lovely and of good report came upon you like a swelling flood. Then you thought of Christ, or afterwards you heard of Christ, and at once you recognized in Him the fullness of all that for which you had dreamed or sighed. He was your One altogether lovely, the chiefest among ten thousand. In Him the vague, wandering aspirations took form and shape. An African savage, who had listened to the missionary's story of the Cross and Him who died thereon, exclaimed, "I always knew that there must be such a Savior!"

We are troubled by the doubts that rise from our own minds, by the unanswerable questions that are flung at us by unbelievers, by the multiplication of sects and the apparently little headway that the Church makes in the world. But let us not forget that the Lord knows them who are His and, what is more, that the sheep hear His voice, that thousands of Christian disciples are finding Christ the One of whose existence their best hopes and aspirations had ever told them; that the deeps in man are ever calling unto the deeps of God, that in Christ men discover their true spiritual homeland.

> Tis the weakness in strength that I cry for! My flesh, that I seek
> In the Godhead! I seek and I find it. O Saul, it shall be
> A Face like my face that receives thee; a Man like to me,
> Thou shalt love and be loved by, forever: a Hand like this hand
> Shall throw open the gates of new life to thee! See the Christ
>   stand!

8

THOMAS

The chief thing to remember about Thomas is not that he doubted, that he asked for unusual evidence, but that he was convinced, that he believed so thoroughly and enthusiastically as to give expression to the greatest confession in Christian history, "My Lord and my God!" (John 20:28).

In connection with Thomas, too often Tennyson's lines,

> There lives more faith in honest doubt,
> Believe me, than in half the creeds,

have been quoted, to the total neglect of the lines that accompany them:

> Perplext in faith, but pure in deeds,
> At last he beat his music out.
>
> He fought his doubts and gather'd strength,
> He would not make his judgment blind,
> He faced the spectres of the mind
> And laid them; thus he came at length
>
> To find a stronger faith his own;
> And Power was with him in the night,
> Which makes the darkness and the light,
> And dwells not in the light alone.

The Psalmist says that God is able to make the wrath of man to praise Him. Here we have an instance of how God can make the doubt of man to praise Him. In the Providence of God, the chief doubter among the apostles becomes the chief defender of the truth of the Resurrection. The history of Thomas disposes effectually of the foolish, and yet much exploited, idea that the disciples were a band of silly enthusiasts, ready to believe anything that their affections should dictate. The disciples were not logicians and schooled in the giving of evidence, but they were not a set of fools; they were hard-headed men, disinclined to believe in the Resurrection, much though they desired to see their Master again.

THOMAS'S TROUBLE

When the women told them of the empty sepulchre and the two men in shining garments, "their words seemed to them as idle tales, and they believed them not" (Luke 24:11). Thomas is the chief representative of this spirit of doubt. In a remarkable manner he was devoted to the Master. When Jesus heard of the sickness of Lazarus and announced to His disciples that He was going to Judea again (He was then beyond the Jordan), they sought to dissuade Him, reminding Him how the Jews of late tried to stone Him. But Thomas, when he saw that Jesus was determined to go, said, "Let us also go, that we may die with Him" (John 11:16).

Who, then, more than this disciple, who was ready to die with Jesus and exhorted His companions to a like loyalty—who more than he could have desired to see Jesus rise again from the dead? But, in spite of that devotion and in spite of that desire, the Resurrection was such a tremendous event that Thomas was sorrowfully skeptical about it. He even, somewhat haughtily, rejected the testimony of his fellow-disciples and declared that he must not only see Christ in the flesh, but that he must examine His wounds so as to establish beyond all peradventure of a doubt that this was his Master who had been crucified. This is the man who, when Jesus meets him, cries out, "My Lord and my God!"

Without any warrant for it whatsoever, Thomas has been called the Rationalist of the Apostolic Band. He is likened to men who claim a superior endowment of intelligence because they set themselves to doubt what others believe. In any company of twelve men where eleven of them believe, the one who doubts will, by his very singularity, attract great attention to himself. The doubters among men have attracted undue attention to themselves, not because of their superior ability, but because of their uniqueness, and too often the desire to dissent is mistaken for convictions grounded upon careful study and superior judgment.

The rationalist, the ordinary skeptic, as we think of him and as we experience him, is not looking for signs of truth in Christianity but for signs of its falsehood. He will ferret out some little seeming discrepancy of the Biblical records and magnify it into a mountain, whereas the mighty panorama of Christian history and influence fades into nothingness. A friend once said to Grant when he was President that Sumner did not believe in the Bible. "Of course," answered General Grant, "Sumner doesn't believe in the Bible. He didn't write it." That attitude of mind towards Christian truth, however justly or unjustly imputed to the brilliant senator from New England, is typical of many of those who vent their doubts loudly and boast that they do not accept anything the way other people do but must have infallible proofs. There are some people who would never believe in any Bible that they themselves did not write.

A DOUBT BORN OF SORROW

Thomas, it is true, asked for signs, for particular evidence, but to liken him to the rationalist, to the skeptic, in the common use of that term is to do him a great injustice and to wrest the Scriptures. The difference between the rationalist and Thomas is this: the rationalist wants to disbelieve; Thomas wanted to believe. The rationalist, of the honest type, is occasioned by study, by examination of evidence, by the pressing bounds of the natural world, making the other world seem unreal; but the doubt of Thomas was the doubt born of sorrow.

This is the deepest doubt of all, the doubt born of sorrow; that is, the doubt which rises out of the experience of our lives. The great doubts are not those that are born in Germany, in the study of the critic, in the debate of religions, nor are they born in the laboratory, from the study of the laws of nature; they are not born of meditating over the rocks and the stars and the planets, of tracing out genealogies and chronologies; they are born in the library and in the laboratory of the soul; they are the dark interrogations cast by the experiences through which we pass in this strange adventure men call life.

The doubt of a man who talks of the impossibility of a Virgin Birth is one thing; but let it not be confused with the doubt of a mother who has lost her firstborn child and wonders if God is, and if her child still lives. The doubt of a man who questions the Mosaic account of the Creation of the world is one thing, but let it not be confused with the doubt of the man who sees the world in travail and sore anguish, the ceaseless invasion of hate and the eternal enmity of the evil for the good, the inhumanity of man to man, and wonders if God has forsaken His world.

The doubt of Thomas was not that of a quibbler, of a cold-blooded, dilettante student; it was the doubt of a man who had lost his Lord and Master. Sorrow had filled his heart. Had his doubt been of that former nature, mere asking for signs or proofs, Jesus would have answered him as He did those other doubters, calling them a wicked and adulterous generation, seeking after a sign. Thomas was not a Sadducee; there is no evidence that he disbelieved in the resurrection as it was commonly held in Israel at that time, that is, he was no professional doubter in a resurrection. But when he was confronted with the death of Jesus, the doubt of sorrow overwhelmed him.

On no other ground can we understand the exquisite, tender manner in which Jesus dealt with him, giving him all that he asked. Nor do I think that Thomas searched the wounds of his Master, as he had declared he must do before he could or would believe. The majestic presence of the Risen Christ like a flood swept away all his doubts and, falling at His feet, he cried in adoration, in belief and in penitence, "My Lord and my God!"

THE TRUE THOMAS

The greatness of Leonardo's conception of the Twelve grew upon me as I studied it from day to day. And among all these masterly representations, I think that of Thomas is *facile princeps*. Look into his face and at once you have the true Thomas, not the Sadducee, the rationalist, the carping critic, but the man of intense affection, but with that earnest, yearning nature touched with the pale cast of melancholy.

Things troubled Thomas that did not trouble other disciples. But Jesus stooped to his infirmity. As if He anticipated the over-praise of Thomas as a skeptic and the neglect of him as a believer, and an undue valuation for the proof of signs and demonstration, Jesus said to Thomas, "Thomas, because thou hast seen Me, thou hast believed: blessed are they that have not seen, and yet have believed" (John 20:29). Jesus did not mean to discount intelligent faith, nor did He put a premium upon easy, unquestioning faith. Nor did He mean to teach that future believers who could not have the evidence afforded Thomas would be happier, more blessed in their faith than was Thomas. It would be difficult to conceive of any Christian more happy, more blessed, more convinced, than was Thomas when he fell at the feet of Christ with his memorable confession.

In that prophecy of the bliss of future believers, Jesus both set the superior worth of evidence that is not founded on visible manifestations—seeing the Lord in the flesh, beholding His wounds— the evidence of faith and the witness of the Spirit, and foretold the joy and happiness which would be the lot of those who hereafter should believe on His Name.

The experience of Thomas is "useful," as Dr. Robert Ellis Thompson writes, "but not ideal." It is not ideal, for we cannot have that kind of evidence for which Thomas asked, neither is that kind of evidence the highest. Christian faith is more than an infallible demonstration: it is the loving venture of the heart, our trust in Christ. What that experience is, and how related to the other, let quaint old Sir Thomas Browne tell us in the sentences of the *Religio Medici*:

> As for those wingy mysteries in divinity, and airy subtleties in religion, which have unhinged the brains of better heads, they never stretched the *pia mater* of mine. Methinks there be not impossibilities enough in religion for an active faith: the deepest mysteries ours contains have not only been illustrated, but maintained, by syllogism and the rule of reason. I love to lose myself in a mystery; to pursue my reason to an *O altitudo*! 'Tis my solitary recreation to pose my apprehension with those involved enigmas

and riddles of the Trinity, Incarnation and Resurrection. I can
answer all the objections of Satan and my rebellious reason with
that odd resolution I learned of Tertullian, *Certum est quia im-
posibile est.* I desire to exercise my faith in the most difficult point;
for, to credit ordinary and visible objects is not faith, but persua-
sion. Some believe the better for seeing Christ's sepulcher; and,
when they have seen the Red Sea, doubt not of the miracle. Now,
contrarily, I bless myself and am thankful that I lived not in the
days of miracles; that I never saw Christ nor His disciples. I would
not have been one of those Israelites that passed the Red Sea; nor
one of Christ's patients, on whom He wrought His wonders: then
had my faith been thrust upon me; nor should I enjoy that greater
blessing pronounced to all that believe and saw not. 'Tis an easy
and necessary belief, to credit what our eye and sense hath examined. I believe He was dead, and buried, and rose again; and desire
to see Him in His glory, rather than to contemplate Him in His
cenotaph or sepulcher. Nor is this much to believe; as we have
reason, we owe this faith unto history: they only had the advan-
tage of a bold and noble faith, who lived before His coming, who,
upon obscure prophecies and mystical types, could raise a belief
and expect apparent impossibilities.

9

JOHN

If there is any failure in the sketches which make up the painting of the Last Supper, I feel that that failure is St. John. Leonardo da Vinci succeeds least of all with that disciple who is the greatest and most gifted personality in the entire group. There is hardly a fault that we can find with his conception of Peter, Judas, Philip, James or the rest. But he has represented John as a full-faced, effeminate youth, with something of a Mona Lisa smile on his lips, his white hands meekly and languidly clasped together, and his head inclined towards Judas, around whose shoulder Peter, with the knife in his right hand, is beckoning to John to ask Jesus whom He meant when He said that one of them should that night betray Him. There is, perhaps, the suggestion of a dreamy introspection, but very little to suggest the John of the Apocalypse, whose emblem is the eagle flying, like John's great angel, in the sun and "kindling his undazzled eye at the full midday beam"; and nothing at all to suggest that blazing Son of Thunder who wished to call down fire on the inhospitable Samaritan village, immortal for its incivility, and who, although he could employ the terms of love and affection, knew how to call the enemies of truth and of Christ "liars" and warn the Church against them.

Jesus loved John. Four times in the Gospel of John we have him described as the disciple whom Jesus loved. Did He not love the others? We know that He did, for John himself in his report of the last night with Christ tells how, "having loved His own which were in the world, He loved them unto the end" (John

13:1). What, then, are we to make of this oft-repeated statement about the regard that Jesus had for John? The only explanation is that on the side of His human nature Jesus gave full play to His natural affections, but in a way that never excites the anger or the jealousy of the disciples.

JESUS AND JOHN

Peter, James and John enjoyed a peculiar intimacy, and John had a place all to himself. There was something in the youth that attracted Jesus and made easy the exchange of spirit. We think of John as the one who, above all the rest, had deep spiritual insight and a quick and easy apprehension of the mystery of God in Christ. These traits appear in his Gospel and his Epistles, and it may have been because he was the first to catch the meaning of Christ, to understand how He was the Eternal Son of God and how He came to give life, that Jesus showed unusual affection for him. We like those who get our meaning quickly, whose thoughts range in the same atmosphere, and who do not, like Philip, need to have every step and every figure explained.

But another explanation of the marked affection which Jesus bore to John may lie in the altogether probable fact that John was the Benjamin of this family of disciples. As such Leonardo represents him, a youth among middle-aged men. Since the record generally reads, not John and James, but James and John, the inference is that John was a younger brother. It is possible too that there was a wide gap between James and John, for even in households today it would not be difficult to find brothers who are separated by almost a score of years. He was certainly younger than Peter and easily outran him on the way to the sepulcher. It may have been because of his youth that he was permitted to pass unchallenged into the court of Annas the high priest. St. John's explanation is that he was "known unto the high priest"; but this need not dismiss the fact that his youth made them pay little attention to him, while Peter had to stay without until John spoke in his behalf and brought him in.

Beyond all this is the very trustworthy tradition that John lived to extreme old age, finally ending his witness on earth in the time of Trajan. The youngest member of any large family is the object of a great deal of advice and commands on the part of his seniors, but also of affection. The mere fact that he is the youngest makes them look upon him a little differently from the way they do upon one another. In times of illness and sorrow there is a medicine in the unconscious ministry of little children; and in grave and serious days of waiting or watching, of famine, or siege, full-grown men relieve their spirits by friendly companionship with youth. The innocence, the guilelessness, the enthusiasm of youth constitutes a balm for the anxiety and strain of maturity.

I like to think of John as playing such a part in the band of apostles. For that reason Jesus loved him, and probably all the others too. St. Paul surrounded himself with a bodyguard of young men, Timothy, Titus, Demas. Our churches need the crown of glory which comes with the gray head. At the communion season we like to see the men who have been through the storms and trials of life stand reverently by the table with its "snowy cloth" and receive from the minister the sacred elements and then give them to the people. But these men once were young; their faith dates back half or three-quarters of a century; and therefore it is that in the midst of the grave and reverend seniors we like to see the inexperience and hopefulness and glowing ardor of youth. The Church should represent in its ministry the full range of human life childhood, youth, middle life and old age.

YOUTH AND OLD AGE

The John whom we see in the Gospels is a youth; but the John who wrote the Apocalypse and the Gospel and the Letters is a full-grown man, perhaps an aged man. It is altogether probable that when John died, the last of all those who had accompanied with Jesus from the beginning, from the time of the preaching of John the Baptist, had passed from the earth. Browning's *Death in the Desert* is the poet's imagination of what John might have said, or ought to have said, when he was dying. On the whole, the poem does gross injustice to him who spoke so cleverly and wrote so simply, and for lucidity of thought and simplicity of style, Browning had studied John to no purpose. But here and there he makes John say something sensible and comprehensible. One instance is

where John refers to his great age and how when he dies the last
eye-witness will be gone:

> If I live yet, it is for good, more love
> Through men to men: be naught but ashes here
> That keeps awhile my semblance, who was John—
> Still, when they scatter, there is left on earth
>
> No one alive who knew (consider this!),
> Saw with his eyes and handled with his hands
> That which was from the first the Word of Life.
> How will it be when none more saith, "I saw"?

It is evidently from the vantage point of great age that John
writes when he composes the First Epistle, for he commences by
saying, "That which was from the beginning, which we have heard,
which we have seen with our eyes, which we have looked upon, and
our hands have handled of the Word of Life . . . that which we have
seen and heard declare we unto you, that ye also may have fellowship with us" (1 John 1:1, 3). But at length the day had to come for
the Church when the last prop of this sort fell away and it had to
stand by its own inner strength and by the word of tradition.

"How will it be when none more saith, 'I saw'?"

Jesus Himself has answered that question, for John writes in his
Gospel how Jesus said to Thomas, "Because thou hast seen Me,
thou hast believed; blessed are they that have not seen and yet
have believed" (John 20:29).

A PUNISHING PORTRAIT

It is a remarkable thing that John, who is so retiring and mod-
est about speaking of himself, never once calling himself by name
in the Gospel, but always either speaking of himself in the third
person or hiding his identity by a phrase such as "the disciple
whom Jesus loved"—should never once refer to any of those incidents in the story of his discipleship which give an unfavorable
impression of his character. That there were such incidents we
know from the other Gospels. Upon three different occasions
John spoke or acted so as to bring upon him the rebuke of Jesus.

Mark tells us that after Jesus had given the disciples an illustrated sermon on humility by taking a child in His arms, John came to him and said that they had seen a man casting out evil spirits in the Name of Jesus and that they had forbidden him. Very likely John or James did the forbidding. John expects Jesus to commend him, but Jesus rebuked him, saying, "There is no man which shall do a miracle in My Name, that can lightly speak evil of Me. For he that is not against us, is on our part" (Mark 9:39,40). The incident reminds one of a similar occasion in the time of Moses. "And the Lord came down in a cloud, and spake unto him, and took of the spirit that was upon him and gave it unto the seventy elders; and it came to pass, that, when the spirit rested upon them, they prophesied, and did not cease. But there remained two of the men in the camp, the name of the one was Eldad, and the name of the other Medad; and the spirit rested upon then; and they were of them that were written, but went not out unto the tabernacle: and they prophesied in the camp. And there ran a young man, and told Moses, and said, Eldad and Medad do prophesy in the camp. And Joshua the son of Nun, the servant of Moses, one of his young men, answered and said, My Lord Moses, forbid them. And Moses said unto him, Enviest thou for my sake? Would God that all the Lord's people were prophets, and that the Lord would put his spirit upon then'!" (Numbers 11:25-29).

SON OF THUNDER?

John had the spirit of exclusiveness which has misrepresented Christ to the world. He was of the spirit of Joshua who would have no prophesying outside of the sacred precinct, which was not according to the common usage, and called upon Moses to suppress it. The noble answer of Moses was a prophecy of the answer of Jesus to John and a prophecy of the answer of Paul fifteen hundred years after Moses, when the Jews were so frightened because Christ was being preached outside their church and custom, "What then? notwithstanding, every way, whether in pretense or in truth, Christ is preached; and I therein do rejoice, yea, and will rejoice" (Phil. 1:18).

Another instance of the narrow spirit of John was his joining with James in asking power to call down fire on the Samaritan village which had showed incivility to their Master. It was the abuse of that which was good. Jesus liked the mercurial, blazing disposition of these two brothers, but His labor was to train them and refine them so that they could use this splendid quality of righteous indignation to better purposes. John never altogether lost those qualities which made Jesus call him a Son of Thunder. Such a man was best fitted to be the medium through which should come the fearful revelation of the symbols of Divine wrath and judgment. It was to the Son of Thunder, not to Leonardo's simpering weakling, that the Lord showed the "things that must shortly come to pass."

Tradition tells us, though uncertainly, that John, too, suffered martyrdom, thus drinking the cup that he said, so eagerly, he was able to drink, but understanding now far better the meaning of the cup and the way to honor and distinction in the Kingdom of Heaven. There are beautiful legends, too, about John tracing a former young disciple, who had fallen away and become chief of a robber band, to his fastness and winning him back to Christ; and of his hurrying from the bath in which he had discovered Cerinthus the heretic, lest the roof should fall upon him; of his tame partridge and of his oft-repeated blessing, when borne by the strong arms of his young men into the Christian assemblage, he lifted his withered arms and said, "Little children, love one another."

John Milton has a great passage in which he gives us his idea of what the character of a poet ought to be. He says: "He who would not be frustrated of his hope to write well ought himself to be a true poem—not presuming to sing high praises of heroic men and women or famous cities, unless he have in himself the experience and practice of all that which is praiseworthy."

BACK OF THE BOOK

In the Apocalypse John gives us the vision of the future. Many of the symbols and emblems perplex and puzzle us; but always the book is radiant with the light of moral splendor. Back of the great book was the great life of the Apostle. As in the book the thunders of judgment alternate with the overtures of mercy and the accents of peace, so in the life of John there was rainbow round about the throne. A veritable Son of Thunder, yet tender and affectionate, leaning upon the breast of Jesus and taking into his arms the weeping Mary with the sword through her heart, and faithless

Peter too. If to John much was given, let it be remembered that John loved much. If to John was granted the vision of the things of the future, unfolding the majesty and the glory, the judgments and the mercy of God, let it be remembered that John was himself in the Spirit when the vision came to him. His holy life was the preparation for the glorious vision. It is John who preserves for us the word of Jesus that if any man love Him He will come unto him. He is the illustration of that promise. "Love only knoweth whence it came, and comprehendeth love."

"Beloved, let us love one another: for love is of God; and everyone that loveth is begotten of God, and knoweth God. He that loveth not knoweth not God, for God is love" (1 John 4:7,8). In "The Last Supper" Leonardo da Vinci puts John at the right hand of Jesus and James at the left. They wished to occupy in Christ's kingdom seats similarly located. Perhaps the Father has given them their petition. We know, at least, that Christ sitteth at the right hand of the Father, and not far from Christ, I doubt not, we shall find him who sat so near to Him upon earth, and who more than any of the apostles has manifested to the world the mind that was in Christ Jesus. Peter, Paul and John—these three are the ones I should look for first when entering heaven.

THE GREATEST GOSPEL?

When Peter asked Jesus what was to happen to the disciple whom Jesus loved, the Master replied, "If I will that he tarry until I come what is that to thee?" (John 21:22). There have been those who, in the light of subsequent Christian history, have interpreted the words of Jesus to mean that until Christ comes, the greatest witness to Him will be the Gospel that John wrote. "His Gospel," writes Schaff, "is the golden sunset of inspiration and sheds its luster into the second and all succeeding centuries of the Church." We have not read many verses of the prologue before we realize that we are dealing with a very great document, not only, as with the other Gospels, because of the great facts set forth, but because of the discussion of the meaning of the facts. When John writes, the first blush of the Christian enthusiasm has commenced to fade and the age of interpretation and theology has commenced.

I venture to say that if the average Christian takes up the Gospels one by one and tries to read them through at a sitting, he will find that the Gospel of John will weary him sooner than any of them. This is due to the fact that the Gospel is made up, for the most part, of a series of discourses of Jesus growing out of incidents in His ministry. Let me enumerate these discourses: Nicodemus and the New Birth, chapter 3; The Woman of Samaria and the Water of Life, chapter 4; The Man Having an Infirmity, chapter 5; Feeding the Four Thousand and the Bread of Life, chapter 6; The Feast of Tabernacles and the Water of Life, chapter 7; Tabernacles and the Light of the World, chapter 8; Spiritual Freedom, 8:31; The Man Born Blind and the Good Shepherd, chapters 9 and 10; The Feast of Dedication and the Love of God and the Jews, chapter 10:22; Greeks and Jews and the Light of the World, chapter 12:20-50; The Last Supper, chapters 14 to 17, containing the discourse of Comfort and the Holy Spirit, the one on Christian Love, the allegory of the vine, and the intercessory prayer.

With all the comfort and help that you get out of these discourses there is much in them that is dark, mysterious and inexplicable. The sentiment in your mind is very often precisely that to which His hearers, whether His own disciples or angry Scribes and Pharisees, gave expression, "What does He mean?" We hear Him tell Nicodemus about the new birth and we say, "How can these things be?" We hear Him tell the Jews that "except ye eat the flesh of the Son of man and drink His blood, ye have no life in yourselves," and with the Jews we say, "How can this man give us His flesh to eat?" Or with the disciples, "This is a hard saying, who can hear it?" Even in that touching farewell address, how much there is amid those blessed sentences of comfort and hope which are still enigmas to you and me. We sympathize with Thomas when he interrupted Christ and said, "We know not whither Thou goest, and how can we know the way?" "In that day," said Christ, "ye shall ask Me no question" (John 16:23, R.V).. That day has not yet come, and still many of these sayings of Christ are what He Himself termed them, "dark sayings" (John 16:25, R.V).

Least of all to our taste are those prolonged discussions which Jesus had with the Jewish leaders at Jerusalem about His rank, His relationship to the Father and His relationship to the world. There Christ appears more as a theological antagonist than as the Great

Teacher and Physician of the other Gospels. This raises what has been called the Johannine problem, the problem of the relationship of this Fourth Gospel to the other three. The problem is stated, though on the side of unbelief, by Renan, who, in the introduction to *The Life of Jesus*, says of the Fourth Gospel, "The mystic tone of these discourses does not correspond at all to the character of the eloquence of Jesus, such as we picture it according to the synoptics. A new spirit has breathed; Gnosticism has already commenced; the Galilean era of the Kingdom of God is finished; the hope of the near advent of Christ is more distant; we enter on the barrenness of metaphysics, into the darkness of abstract dogma."

This is an extreme statement of the case; but even the most reverent believer will oftentimes be puzzled when he listens to the Jesus of these polemical discourses with the Jews and turns from them to the Sermon on the Mount as Matthew recorded it. A favorite explanation of the authorship of the Gospel has been that some Alexandrine Christian, a disciple of Philo, wrote the Gospel but used Jesus as the mouthpiece for his sublime speculations in much the same way that Plato makes use of Socrates to press his ideas.

The solution of the difficulty is probably to be sought in the fact that John is not making any special effort to reproduce verbatim the sayings of Jesus, but mold them into his own thought and expression. And, different as the style of these addresses in the Fourth Gospel are, we have no difficulty at all in discerning in them the same Christ whom we see in the other Gospels. Much of the difference in tone and manner is to be accounted for by the difference in aim that John had, not primarily to write a narrative of the life of Jesus, for that had been well done, but to gather together proofs of His divinity and Messiahship.

JOHN AND PAUL

The Eternal Logos of John and the Incarnate Son of God occupies the same place that is ascribed to Him in the writings of St. Paul. One might take the Letter to the Colossians and say there was nothing there in common with the Christ of the first three disciples, but Paul writes, as in many places John does, from a theological standpoint. We know from the letters of Paul and the other writings of John that the Christian faith was being obscured by strange and fantastic speculations. It cannot be said that the Fourth Gospel is directed against any one of these, but certain corruptions of the Christian truth seem always to lie in the background, and John probably had them in mind. His Gospel lives up to its confessed aim, to prove the divinity of Jesus. It is a clear-cut statement of the fundamental truth of Christianity that the Son of God became man, taking to Himself a true body and a reasonable soul.

As long as Christians hold to that they have a peculiar and glorious religion. As soon as they forget it, they begin to fall into the morass of pantheism, and the various other isms and cults that have sprung up like Cadmus' teeth. That Jesus is the Eternal Son of God, that He became flesh and dwelt among us, that He died on the Cross for our sins, that He rose from the dead, that by believing in Him we have life eternal there the whole Christian structure stands or falls. Wherever that is gone, we have only the name of Christianity, but not its substance.

What makes John's Gospel beloved to the Church, however, is not its great apology for the divinity of Jesus Christ, but its ministry of comfort and hope to the disciple's heart. Our Lord's words as He sat by the well of Jacob to the woman of Samaria, "Whosoever drinketh of the water that I shall give him shall never thirst," fall sweetly on the believer's ears, as sweetly as those other words of the Gospel of Matthew, "Come unto Me all ye that labor and are heavy laden, and I will give you rest. Take My yoke upon you; and learn of Me; for I am meek and lowly in heart: and ye shall find rest unto your souls. For My yoke is easy, and My burden is light."

If Luke gives us the parable of the Lost Sheep (Matthew also), it is John who tells us of the Good Shepherd and the sheepfold, and how Christ is the Good Shepherd because He lay down His life for the sheep. The others tell us of Jairus' daughter and the widow of Nain's son, but it is John, in his story of Lazarus and Mary and Martha, who tells the perfect story of the tender pathos of the house of mourning, the heartache of sorrow, touched by the hope of life eternal.

JESUS' LAST WORDS

But most precious of all is what the writer of the hymn has called "His tender last farewell." This farewell address and last prayer are preserved for us by John in the last part of his Gospel. If we wonder why he forsook Galilee's shores for the precincts of the temple and preferred the disputes between Jesus and the Pharisees as to His nature and claims to those other sayings of Jesus about purity and meekness and patience and kindness—we can never be thankful enough that he preserved for us the last words of Jesus to His disciples and the great prayer which He offered for Himself, for the whole Church in every age and among every people. There we hear the new commandment that we love one another, "even as I have loved you." There our relationship to Him is described under the beautiful figure of the vine and its branches, "I am the vine, ye are the branches."

There the promise of the Holy Spirit's presence and guidance in the Church is given. There is the solemn prophecy of suffering and tribulation in this world, but also the assurance of victory through Him who has overcome the world. There we hear Him pray for the unity of the Church, "that they all may be one, as Thou, Father, art in Me, and I in Thee." There we have a vision of the final glory of all who believe, for there Christ prays that we may all be where He is and behold His glory. There, too, we hear the reading of the last will and testament of our Savior, and realize how not as the world giveth, He gives unto us. The world gives unrest, disquiet, but Christ gives peace. "Peace I leave with you; My peace I give unto you."

And there, when sorrow's driving rain beats against the window of the soul, and death's fearful victory and piercing sting seem to have written across all our hopes and occupations and yearnings and achievements and affections, one dark word, "Vanity," and fears are in the way, and all the daughters of life's music are brought low—we hear those words at which arms grow strong again and hearts grow brave, those most loved by His Church of all the words of life that fell from Immanuel's lips—"Let not your heart be troubled; ye believe in God, believe also in Me. In My Father's house are many mansions; if it were not so, I would have told you. I go to prepare a place for you. And if I go and prepare a place for you, I will come again and will receive you unto Myself; that where I am, there ye may be also."

10

JAMES, THE FIRST TO DIE

Seventeen years before this day of his execution, James and his brother John had asked for seats of honor in the kingdom of Christ. Jesus asked them if they were ready to pay the price. Could they be baptized with His baptism? Could they drink His cup? Eagerly and impulsively, if ignorantly, they had answered, "We are able." Now for James the final test had come. Over him flashed the persecuting sword of Herod Agrippa, the brother of that Herodias who had been the cause of the death of John the Baptist. The bitter chalice was pressed to the lips of James and he drank it in the faith and spirit of His Master. James was not

> The martyr first, whose eagle eye
> Could pierce beyond the grave,
> Who saw his Master in the sky,
> And called on Him to save,

for the distinction of wearing the first martyr's crown belongs to the pious and eloquent Stephen. But the first of the apostles to die was James. Hence he is called the proto-martyr. The lips of the evangelist are sealed as to the manner of the death of James. We would like to think, indeed we can think, that this James, who once asked permission to call down fire on bigoted and inhospitable Samaritans, knew better now the spirit that he was of, and that, softened and purified by the memories of Jesus, he went to his death like Stephen with a prayer for "them that did the wrong."

It is very singular that James' own brother John never once mentions him in his long Gospel, nor aside from the story of his martyrdom do we hear of him in the book of the Acts, save in a catalogue of the apostles. We might dismiss him as one of the least important of the Twelve; but the fact of his being picked out for the sword by Herod shows that James occupied a most notable position as an apostle. Herod killed him in order to please the Jews, and in selecting his victim he would choose an outstanding figure in the band of Christian disciples. Moreover, the next apostle whom he marked for the slaughter was none other than Peter. The silence, then, of John and the comparative silence of the Acts is not to be taken to mean that James was not a leading figure in the band of apostles.

FIRST TO DIE

He was the first of the Twelve to taste of death. Judas tasted of death even before Christ was crucified; but now we leave him out of the reckoning and, counting Matthias in the place of Judas, James is, apart from all personal traits, brought prominently before us because of the Twelve he was the first to die. The first to die! This was a band of friends, a family, as it here. Now death invades that home and the one for whom he calls first is James.

Sometimes it is John, sometimes Peter, sometimes Henry, sometimes Robert, sometimes Mary, sometimes Sarah—but always there is a first. Strong, rugged brothers grow and thrive and toil for long years and never think of death as a thing related to them. Then one day comes the tidings, "James is very sick; James died last night." So runs the history of all families, of all earthly groups and associations, of all graduating classes—always a first to feel the edge of death's sharp sword. Oh thank God for families! If you have had brothers and sisters and are blessed with many of them, thank Heaven for it and show your gratitude by kindness to your own.

All that John and Peter and Matthew and the rest could do when they heard that James was dead was to take up his body and give it decent sepulchre. Did they think now of any kindness they might have shown James? Did John recall how he might have been a little more thoughtful concerning that elder brother of his?

Was there anything that ought to have been done before Herod's sword flashed and fell? We do not know. But if there were, it could now never, never be done. In this matter, in this great matter of family relationship, the duties and privileges of brothers and friends, whatsoever your hand finds to do, do it now and with all your might.

With your might! Life's transitoriness and brevity demand all your might in this matter, for when the sword of the inevitable and inexorable Herod of Death falls, then all your might and all your tears and repentance will avail nothing!

Comparing Matthew 27:56 with Mark 15:40, we are justified in thinking that the "mother of the sons of Zebedee" and Salome are one and the same person. In St. John's list of the women at the Cross (John 19:25), "His mother's sister" is mentioned. It has been conjectured that this was Salome, and thus James and John would be cousins of Jesus.

We know that James' mother was a strong-minded woman, ambitious for her sons, for although Mark says that James and John made the request that they might sit, one on the right hand and the other on the left of Jesus in His Kingdom, St. Matthew says that the request was made through their mother.

Remarkable men have back of them remarkable mothers, and Salome must have been such a woman. She was at fault in the manner of her request, nevertheless it was a place in the Kingdom of Christ that she asked for her children; it was near Him that she yearned to see her sons. Bathsheba desired for her son Solomon the throne of Israel. Agrippina, the mother of Nero, poisoned Claudius and Britannicus that her son might wear the purple. In his powerful drama "Nero," Stephen Phillips, that magician of our English words, dead before his prime, makes Agrippina say:

> Mothers for children have dared much and more
> Have suffered; but what mother hath so scarred
> Her soul for the dear fruit of her body as I?
> I have made a way for thee through ghosts.
>
> Witness if easily my son did reign;
> I am bloody from head to foot for sake of him,
> And for my cub am I incarnadined.

THE WAY OF MOTHERS

We should all occupy high stations in life were the things that mothers ask for their sons granted them. What did your mother wish for you? I know that she held you in her arms and wished that some of the honors and distinctions of this world might be bestowed upon you, for our mothers always fondly believe that for us, their sons, is all that is desirable in Israel. And very often mothers wish for their sons places and honors which they are not fitted to occupy or to wear. But there is one maternal wish and ambition that all good mothers cherish, and for which all sons are by nature fitted or can be made fit, and that is to be upright in soul, to be unstained by this world, to be a friend of Christ.

O calm, patient mothers, some of you living and some of you living with God, you have blessed and refreshed humanity because you did wish for your sons, not riches and honors and fame and this world's glory, but that they might seek first the Kingdom of God and His righteousness! Your sons get well on into the stream of life; they reach some honors and others they miss altogether despite their wishes and their struggles; they gain riches here or lose them yonder; they see some dreams come true and others never fulfilled—vast, many-turreted, palace-walled mirages of glorious colors that faded dismally away upon the desert's face as they drew nigh to possess them. At length, O desiring mothers, they do begin to understand that when you wished for them purity of heart, freedom from the stain of this world, that they might have riches in heaven, that they might wear the decorations of Jesus Christ, you did most truly wish for them the real, the abiding, the time-defying, the death-scorning honors and high places and possessions!

JAMES' FATHER

But what of James' father? Zebedee was his name, a prosperous fish merchant of Capernaum. His class was good. As Principal Adeny says of his sons, he "came from that vigorous lower middle class which has furnished so many effective workers for the cause of God and humanity in all ages—a class not so far removed from the danger of want as to be able to relax its energies and sink down into self-indulgence, but yet not so bound down to drudgery as to lose heart and inspiration for subjects beyond the daily routine of toil."

Salome became one of the women who attended Jesus upon His journeys, supported Him with their substance, stood afar off beholding His Cross and wept at His sepulcher; but of Zebedee we hear nothing further. We like to think that he, too, became a disciple of Jesus and that this James is a representative of one of those Christian homes in which all the members are followers of the Lamb. It is a blessed thing when it is so. Who, having once tasted, can speak lightly of the joy of being in a home where father and mother, brothers and sisters are all friends of Christ?

Robert Burns strikes this note when he makes the old father in *The Cotter's Saturday Night* thus pray to heaven for the redemption of all his children and their reunion in heaven:

> Then kneeling down to Heaven's Eternal King,
> The saint, the father and the husband prays:
> Hope "springs exulting on triumphant wing,"
> That thus they all shall meet in future days,
> There, ever bask in uncreated rays,
> No more to sigh, or shed the bitter tear,
> Together hymning their Creator's praise,
> In such society, yet still more dear;
> While circling time moves round in an eternal sphere.

James was one of three disciples admitted to a special intimacy with Christ. He saw Him transfigured, he saw Him raise the dead, he was taken apart with Him in Gethsemane. Yet James, as well as Peter and John, frequently manifests a spirit that had little to do with that of Christ. The most striking instance of this was when a Samaritan village refused to show Jesus hospitality or grant a place to rest because He and His companions were Jews. This insult brought to the surface all the flaming wrath of the Sons of Thunder, and they requested permission to call down fire from heaven upon the inhospitable village.

The descendants of James and John have been legion. They have done what Jesus did not permit these fiery apostles to do; they have called down flames of devastation and destruction upon those races and creeds and nations and cities which refused to receive them or adopt their opinions. Whenever I see the flame of martyrs' pyres, the persecution of Jews and Turks by Christians, the fierce intolerance of sects within the Church, the sad instances of divisions within the local churches, the savage anathema of systems of theology which claim absolute truth, or the personal bitterness which makes one man hate another, the ferocious insistence upon petty details of modes of worship or interpretations of the Bible as modes of baptism, orders of ordination and practices of the Lord's Supper, yes, in the conflicts of race with race and nation with nation, one race or one nation claiming the right to rule another and telling it to submit or be damned, annihilated—there I see the reflection of that evil spirit which flamed in the faces of John and James when they asked permission to call down fire from heaven upon the little village of Samaria, nameless but immortal for its incivility.

Ever I seem to hear the sad refrain of those words of Jesus, as He stands invisibly present by every burning village and smoking city, by the side of every poor wretch for his faith stretched on the rack or tortured with flames, in every conclave of Protestants excommunicating other sects and commanding men to take their way to the Kingdom of Heaven or be damned, every congregation where men in His Name state their opinions regarding obscure passages in the Bible or practices of worship, insisting that he is no Christian who does not as they do—ever I seem to hear the sad refrain, "Ye know not what manner of Spirit ye are of, for the Son of Man is not come to destroy men's lives, but to save them" (Luke 9:55:56).

ABRAHAM'S VISITOR

There is an old legend of Abraham which teaches its lesson of toleration. Sitting one day at the door of his tent, he was visited by a stranger. Abraham asked him within and they sat down to break bread together. Unlike Abraham, the stranger did not pause to ask a blessing. Abraham inquired the reason why, and he told him that he worshipped the sun. Angry with him, Abraham drove him out of the tent. Afterwards the Lord called and asked where the stranger was. Abraham replied, "I thrust him out because he did not worship Thee." Then said the Lord: "I have suffered him and his ancestors for hundreds of years, and couldst not thou endure him for one hour?"

When we grow angry with those who differ with us, impatient of differing sects of Protestants, or loud-mouthed, bigoted unbelievers, wishing them eliminated from the families of the earth, let us remember that God has suffered them, yea, that He has suffered generation after generation of sinners upon the face of the earth. We can afford to be as tolerant as God.

> For the love of God is broader
> Than the measures of man's mind,
>   And the heart of the Eternal
> Is most wonderfully kind:
>   But we make His love too narrow
> By false limits of our own,
>   And we magnify His strictness
> With a zeal He will not own.

Newman used to pray that the people of England might become more intolerant. He meant, of course, not that they would set to harrying one another for their faith again, but that Christians would take more seriously the faith they held. The danger today is not always that of intolerance; it is quite frequently the danger of indifference. If men are in earnest about their faith they will contend for it. Christ did not choose weaklings for the inner band of His friends, but strong, mercurial, impulsive men. James and John He surnamed Boanerges, Sons of Thunder. Sometimes their ardor carried them too far, as in this instance of the Samaritan village; but within bounds it was a noble and worthy trait, this ability to be volcanic, to thunder, to talk like Elijah.

"He was incapable of moral indignation" was the comment made upon one of our American ambassadors who died some time ago. He was a gifted man, but Jesus would never have chosen him for the apostolate. The highest manhood must be capable of indignation, it must know how to kindle and flare with righteous anger. Better the misdirected zeal of James and John than the smiles and caresses of the indifferent.

Anger is a great virtue; even God is represented as at times an angry God. That means that man and God can feel deeply. But anger uncontrolled, or not evoked by just occasion, is a menace to the soul and can do injury wherever its flame consumes. Be angry, but sin not. But do not fear to be a Son of Thunder. Christ desired such men for His disciples. I have no doubt that the reason why the Jews desired the death of James before all the other apostles, and therefore why Herod chose him for the sword, was because James had spoken great, plain, burning words there in Jerusalem, such as only a Son of Thunder knew how to speak. As Carlyle wrote of John Knox, "Tolerance has to tolerate the unessential and see well what that is. Tolerance has to be noble, just, measured in its wrath, when it can tolerate no longer. But on the whole, we are not here altogether to tolerate. We are here to resist, to control, to vanquish withal. We do not tolerate Falsehoods, Thieveries, Iniquities, when they fasten upon us; we say to them, Thou art false, thou art not tolerable!"

11

PETER

They were all human, these men whom Jesus called to follow Him; but Peter reveals more of himself than any of the others, and the self that he shows is so remarkably like the self that followers of Jesus today see in themselves that I venture to name Peter the most human of the Apostles. We know far more about Peter, both in the Gospels and out of them, than we do of any other disciple. He speaks more frequently than the others and is spoken to frequently by Jesus; the story of the spread of the Church as told in the book of the Acts tells more about what Peter did and said and suffered and where he went than it does about any of the Twelve, or any of the followers of Jesus, save that one whose name and whose deeds were destined to eclipse those of Peter himself.

Not only is Peter the speaker and the actor whom we know best, but when he does speak and act he does so in a manner that is peculiarly self-revelatory. You know persons who speak and act before you, but neither their words nor their actions tell you much about them, the manner of soul that lies beneath that exterior; they are neutral in their conduct, so far as revealing self is concerned. Then there are others who speak and act, but their words and their deeds may be such as give an altogether wrong impression as to their character, deceiving rather than enlightening. But Peter is one of those whole-hearted men who do whatever they do, in good or in evil, with their whole might, leaving no slightest doubt as to the kind of person who is speaking or acting. Peter could not have hidden his real self or disguised himself had he tried to do it. He was a non deliberative, warm-hearted, impulsive, quick-acting soul who was mastered by the motive of the moment, whether it was good or bad. Someone has said that the worst disease of the heart is cold. Peter never had that disease, although he had many other sicknesses of the soul.

THE TYPES OF MANKIND

Take any group of men like these twelve and you will find represented there the types of mankind. Even in a family where there are six or eight, or even four brothers, you will find one who is on the order of Thomas, perhaps, another on the order of James, another who is like Nathanael or like John, and almost always one who is like Peter. In my own family, one of four sons, I had a brother who reminds me of Peter. He was impulsive, affectionate, ready in speech, completely carried away by the enthusiasm of a moment, sometimes boastful as to future accomplishments, sanguine often to the verge of folly, but strong-hearted and strong-minded, awakening in others reciprocal affection and enthusiasm. He had not the balance of another brother, nor the patience of a second, nor the penetration of a third; but these Petrine qualities he possessed to a marked degree. I mention this only to show that it is not difficult to get the measure of Peter. He is one of those men whom we get to know quickly, but who are, notwithstanding, supremely worth knowing.

Even if the Gospels had told us much more about John and James and the others than they do, and yet told us what they have about Peter, I am sure that Peter would be the one we should know the best. His acts and speeches are such as impress themselves upon the mind. He commences his relationship with Jesus, at least at the time of the formal call to become a disciple, by falling at the feet of Jesus in the fishing boat and beseeching Him to depart from him, and ends that earthly exchange with an impulsive and wholly disinterested question about the future of John.

He is the disciple who tries to walk to Jesus on the stormy deep, who would stay with Jesus on the mount of Transfiguration, who will not have Jesus wash his feet, who boasts of his loyalty and then with an oath affirms his disloyalty, who out with a sword and cuts off the ear of Malchus, who brushes aside the hesitating John and goes boldly into the sepulcher, who, when he knows that Jesus is standing on the shore, wraps his fisher's coat about him and plunges into the sea and swims to the shore, unable to wait for the clumsy boats to bring him to Jesus.

What a series of striking utterances and dramatic actions! That leap of his into the sea to get to Christ at once is one of the best commentaries on the character of Peter. There you have Peter at his best—his redeemed self, full of vigor, full of love, full of action, impulsive, daring, overwhelming you with his glad enthusiasm. It was John who first saw Jesus through the dim mists of the morning. His was the intuitive soul that could apprehend the truth of the sayings of Jesus and grasp the place that Christ had in the mystery of redemption; but it was Peter who hurled himself into the sea.

A NATURAL LEADER

A character like Peter's cannot be assumed or counterfeited. Nathanael or John would look very foolish if they tried to act like Peter. This leaping activity of soul and body, this effervescence of spirit must be natural. When it is natural it is admired, when assumed it is laughed at. The mental and physical activity of Peter turns one's mind to the mystery of influence and leadership. It was to this disciple, one who acted and spoke as Peter did, that Jesus gave the leadership; regardless of the claims of Rome, Peter certainly, both in the Gospels and in the Acts, is the leader among the disciples of Jesus. Mere physical alertness and activity have their influence upon the mind of man, and men seem to take naturally to the leadership of those who do not wait for the appointment of leadership, but assume it. Apart, then, from his spiritual endowments and the training which he received from Jesus, Peter had those native physical qualities which are magnetic and draw men to him who possesses them. It is indeed a great gift, but woe to him who tries to put on even a physical alertness and enthusiasm which is not native to him. But the genuine thing as Peter possessed it is one of the foundations of true leadership.

I have adverted to the place given Peter in the Roman Catholic theology. "Thou art Peter, and upon this rock I will build My

Church, and the gates of hell shall not prevail against it" are the
words that are traced about the dome of Peter's Church in Rome.
Not much is to be gained by going over that old discussion as to
the powers conferred upon Peter and his successors by Jesus. But
there is something both natural and unnatural in the place that
Rome has given and now gives to St. Peter. There is a naturalness
in this elevation of Peter, because Christianity claims to be a universal religion and as such must be adapted to men of every kind
of mind and disposition. Peter, more than any of the Apostles, is
the type of the universal man. Paul was the chosen Apostle to the
Gentiles, yet magnificently gifted as he was, he represents a special
type, the devotee, the scholar, the philosopher. So does John the
mystic, so does Bartholomew the dreamer.

Peter was not an average, two-talent man by any means, but he
certainly represents humanity in its length and breadth and depth
and height more than any other Apostle. He was not too dull, nor
was he too gifted, not stupid, nor yet too profound. These traits
come out in his two Letters, which are wonderfully self-revealing.
Indeed, if one were asked to select out of the New Testament a
series of passages best adapted for the guidance of the average
Christian in all parts of the world, in all ages of man, one could
not do better than make a little volume out of the sayings of Peter.
One would omit, of course, his references to the ark and to Christ
preaching to the dead and much of his eschatological thunderings,
not because they have not their place, but because one is looking
for passages which at once will direct and guide the Christian
believer. With the exception of these few portions, where in the
Bible could one secure such a manual for everyday Christian experience? There is a fitness, then, in the Roman elevation of Peter to
a place of representative authority. Take him all in all, he is the
best model and the best teacher for men at large.

What, then, is unnatural in this elevation of Peter to the
primacy? He was that one of the Apostles who was so open-
hearted, so whole-souled, so impulsive, so emotional, so frank,
so sincere, so ingenuous. Strange fate that such an Apostle should
be made the cornerstone of a system so opposite to his own
nature! That Peter with the keys as we see him in the Roman
churches, "the pilot of the Galilee lake" with his "massy keys,"
the head of this system of ecclesiasticism and mystery we know

and care little about; he is so different from the Peter of our Lord and of the New Testament.

PETER'S WIFE

Peter had a wife, and we cannot but wonder what kind of wife she was. She must have been a credit and a help to him, else he had not carried her about with him on his missionary tours as we are told by Paul he did. It had been sad indeed had that splendid enthusiast been compelled to go about with a cold millstone of a wife hung about his eager neck, mocking at his zeal and pointing out his inconsistencies, of which there were probably not a few. We infer, both from this fact that his wife went about with him, and also from the reading of his two Letters, that she was a real benediction to him, for no New Testament writer touches with such adornment the subject of marriage and the duties of husbands towards their wives and of wives toward their husbands.

Paul indeed makes Christ's love for the Church the symbol of the love that men ought to bear to their wives, and a great and moving passage it is; nevertheless, we cannot forget, at least some cannot, that it is Paul who conceives of woman's place in a negative more than a positive sense, dwelling upon what woman is not to do rather than upon what she may do. But it is Peter who makes that tender and lovely, though oft abused, reference to woman as the "weaker vessel" to whom honor is due. What eloquent sermons have been preached upon that text !

From the beginning to the end of his career, as it is sketched for us in the Gospels, Peter is "consistently inconsistent." He hails Jesus as the Son of God and the next moment tries to dissuade Him from His redemptive work, bringing upon himself the rebuke, "Get thee behind Me, Satan!" He believed that Jesus could support him on the swelling waves of Galilee, but his faith forsook him when he found himself beyond the safety of the boat. He protests against Jesus washing his feet and then wants Him to wash not his feet only, but his hands and his feet. He boasted that though all should forsake Jesus, he would be found faithful, and then he denied Him. He cut off the ear of Malchus in the Garden and then forsook Jesus. After his vision on the roof of Simon the tanner, he cast off his Jewish prejudices, but after fraternizing with the Gentile converts at Antioch, withdrew from their company when "certain from James" came down, fearing the censure of that pillar of the Church and his influential party.

Even the Peter of fiction and legend is represented as a man of persistent but noble inconsistency. A few days before the time set for his execution at Rome, he bribed the jailer and escaped from the Mamertine prison. But outside the gates of the city he met his Lord bearing a cross. To Him the surprised Peter said, "*Domi, quo vadis?*" (Lord, whither goest Thou?) Jesus answered, "*Venio Romana iterum crucifigi.*" (I go to Rome to be crucified again). Thus warned and humbled, Peter went back to Rome and presented himself to his jailer to be crucified head downwards. Despite these inconsistencies, Peter holds our affection and our admiration. He deserved the stinging and humiliating rebuke administered to him by Paul at Antioch for refusing to associate with the Gentile Christians, and we cannot think of Paul so acting. Nevertheless, Peter is so transparent in his character, so absolute in his actions both for good and for evil, that we never lose interest in him, and his very inconsistencies commend him to us; for if we take the measure of our Christian life, most of us will find that we fall into the class represented by Peter rather than into that represented by the superior and magnificent Paul.

Think how Peter acted at times in ways that were inconsistent with the weakness, the fear, the cowardice that was in him; he thrills us with the possibilities of life—your life and my life. There is no doubt about the elements of weakness within us, but a life like Peter's tells us that it need not always be so with us, that it is possible to rise above this weaker and worse self into the high powers of another and nobler but not less real self. I can be inconsistent in my goodness with my weakness and sinfulness, by the Spirit of Jesus resting upon me, acting and speaking at times in a way that is contrary to and in utter defiance of what has seemed to be the law of my ordinary life; and each time that I so act, I weaken the authority of that old law, that old man, and add to the authority of the new. It is not that a man has his weaknesses and his peculiar and besetting sins, but that he never accepts their dominion as final and never permits to pass by unused an opportunity of rebelling against their authority that constitutes the great and hopeful thing in man. When Peter goes wrong, he always comes back to the right;

when he falls, he rises again. Although he often goes wrong, he never impresses us as the sort of man who is content to do evil or who despairs of doing good. Have we failed? Have you been so weak that it has cost you shame and bitter tears? Have you done evil when you were planning how you would do good? If so, show by your conduct in the future that you can be noble, inconsistent with that past record, and make your solemn vow that the Christ-inspired and Christ-governed better self that is in you will be seen in action and heard in speech and felt in influence.

> Not in their brightness, but their earthly stain
> Are the true seed vouchsafed to earthly eyes,
> And saints are lowered that the world may rise.

A SAINT IN THE MAKING

At the time of his fall, Peter was a saint only in the sense that he was being trained for a character and a work that would win him that high encomium. But there indeed a saint was in the making, "lowered that the world might rise." No incident in Christian history has been such a source of comfort and warning. Peter's fall has done more to make men Christians than Paul's conversion—I mean, the recital of it. There is no scene in Scripture which so illustrates the weakness of the human heart and our proneness to sin, and at the same time nothing in the Scriptures or in Christian history which manifests so exquisitely the tender, seeking, restoring love of Jesus Christ. Here is all the pathos of sin—man's denial and rejection of the Son of God. Not since our first parents wept at the gates of Eden had such tears been shed as those which coursed down the fisherman's face when he went out into the night after he had heard the cock crow. We are not angry with Peter, nor indeed greatly amazed at his fall. Our first and last feeling is one of sadness. There are writers who can make one weep as they recite the wrongs and the sufferings of mankind; and others who can make one weep with the lover or maid upon whom the tragedy of life has fallen. But the Bible makes man weep over sin. Sin is tragic, terrible, but it is also unutterably sad, pathetic. If you would get an understanding of the pathos of sin, behold the look in the face of Jesus as He turns to look upon Peter when he had denied Him for the third time.

Judas was in despair because of his horror at the stature of the evil one that was in him; Peter was in tears because he realized that the worst and weaker Peter had denied Jesus when all the time the better and stronger Peter, his own best self, had been ready and willing to confess Jesus. His was the sorrow not of a man who had done evil that he had planned and then found his mistake, but the sorrow of a man who had done the very thing he hated and left undone the good he would have done. In his *Tale of Two Cities*, Charles Dickens, in describing the grief of the dissipated but gifted lawyer's clerk, tells of the sorrow that man feels when he has been disloyal to himself, and, like Saul, has cast away his shield as if it had not been anointed with oil.

> When his host followed him out on the staircase with a candle, to light him down the stairs, the day was coldly looking in through its grimy windows. When he got out of the house, the air was cold and sad, the dull sky overcast, the river dark and dim, the whole scene like a lifeless desert. And wreaths of dust were spinning round and round before the morning blast, as if the desert sand had risen far away, and the first spray of it in its advance had begun to overwhelm the city. Waste forces within him, and a desert all around, this man stood still on his way across a silent terrace, and saw for a moment, lying in the wilderness before him, a mirage of honorable ambition, self-denial and perseverance. In the fair city of this vision there were airy galleries from which the loves and graces looked upon him, gardens in which the fruits of life hung ripening, waters of hope that sparkled in his sight. A moment, and it was gone. Climbing to a high chamber in a well of houses, he threw himself down in his clothes on a neglected bed, and its pillow was wet with wasted tears. Sadly, sadly, the sun rose; it rose upon no sadder sight than the man of good abilities and good emotions, incapable of their directed exercise, incapable of his own help and his own happiness, sensible of the blight on him, and resigning himself to let it eat him away.

Between the Peter whom we last see going out into the night to weep his bitter tears and the bold death-scorning Apostle of the New Testament, there stands one mighty transforming fact: the resurrection appearance of Jesus to Peter. The angel at the tomb had indeed sent a special message for Peter. "Go, tell His disciples and Peter" (Mark 16:7). It was as if the sin of Peter had cast him out of the band of the disciples and that none would think of him as being included in a general message for the disciples. But more precious than this message was the appearance. It was too sacred for even the Sacred Page. Something sealed the lips of the evangelists, and Peter himself, usually so outspoken and frank in all that happened to him, has not a word to say of it in his two letters. The scene that is painted by the master hand of St. John in the last two pages of his Gospel, the interview between Jesus and Peter by the seashore, was not the restoration of Peter to the Apostolate. It was but a public record or sanction of what had already taken place when Jesus met Peter, and met him alone. We can imagine what Peter said, or rather what Jesus said, for I think this must have been the one time when impetuous, impulsive Peter had nothing to say and was content to let another do the speaking. It is for the imagination, a sacred and blessed field, but each one of us must think of it and picture it for himself.

PETER THE WRITER

In a less theological and argumentative form than Paul's, but with warm and tender zeal, Peter in his Letters writes of the Atonement for the sins of man through the death of Christ. "Ye were redeemed," he writes, "not with corruptible things, with silver and gold, from your vain manner of life handed down from your fathers; but with precious blood, as of a Lamb without blemish and without spot, even the blood of Christ" (1 Peter 1:18, 19). In the opening note of the doxology, in the first letter, it is difficult not to hear the echo of Peter's own experience— "Blessed be the God and Father of our Lord Jesus Christ, who according to His great mercy begat us again unto a living hope, by the resurrection of Christ from the dead." Was he not thinking how the resurrection of Christ from the dead and His special appearance unto him had been the resurrection of hope in his own heart? The Master he had deserted and denied sought and found him and brought him back into His fold.

"The strongest, whitest, sweetest soul the world has ever known"—thus a celebrated Anglo-American preacher once described Jesus in a New York pulpit. How strange, how very strange, that would sound in a letter of Peter or Paul! They, too, and that in matchless terms, could speak of the lovely traits of the Son of Man. But what constrains their love and indites their song of thanksgiving and gives wings to their hope is not the loveliness of the character of Jesus, but the fact that He died for them and bare their sins in His own Body on the tree. It was belief in that fact that built the Church and that has preserved the Church from the days of Peter down to this present time.

After all these pages about Peter, this last thing that I shall say of him is, perhaps, the main thing to be said, and the most luminous thing: Peter was a sinner who had been saved by what he himself called "the great mercy" of God.

12

JUDAS, WHO BETRAYED HIM

"And as to Judas Iscariot, my reason is different. I would fain see the face of him who, having dipped his hand in the same dish with the Son of Man, could afterwards betray Him. I have no conception of such a thing; nor have I ever seen any picture (not even Leonardo's very fine one) that gave me the least idea of it." So, according to William Hazlitt in his essay on *Persons One Would Wish to Have Seen*, spake Charles Lamb. And so say we all. Could we see his face we might get some idea of the man and some understanding of his crime. Judas is the man of mystery among the Twelve. "I have no conception of such a thing," said Lamb, meaning of a man who could dip his hand in the same dish with Jesus and then betray Him. Judas is the most definitely classified disciple among the Twelve; "who betrayed Him" is the epithet of infamy with which the Gospels hand him down to succeeding generations. Yet how hard it is to conceive of Judas, his call to discipleship, his treason, his remorse, his fearful taking off. The end and the beginning in him perplex and baffle us.

When we come to study him we confront the mystery of pre-destination and man's free will, easily scoffed at and ridiculed, or conveniently dismissed, but in the life of Judas a fact to be reck-oned with, if, indeed, there is any fact presented to us by the Four Gospels. Here, too, we are confronted by the mystery of the Satanic element in human nature, the Satanic, diabolical possibili-ties of the soul of man. "One of you is a devil," said Jesus. And yet He had chosen him. "Satan entered him," wrote John. Yet Judas broke his heart and his body with remorse for his sin against the Son of God.

THE MAN OF MYSTERY

In the introduction to the widely read missionary biography, *Mary Slessor of Calabar*, W. P. Livingstone writes as follows: "Life for most people is governed by authority and convention, but behind these there lies the mystery of human nature, uncertain and elusive, and apt, now and again, to go off at a tangent and disturb the somewhat smooth working of organized routine." It is this mystery of human nature that we feel when we take up the character of Judas Iscariot, the mystery of evil, primarily, but also the mystery of good, for although Judas died by his own hand in a fit of despair, that despair was the fruit of remorse. If the crime of Judas perplexes us—how a man could do it, betray Jesus with a kiss, and for a paltry sum—still more does his remorse perplex us. A man, according to all experience, who could commit such an abnormal crime ought to have been too bad a man to suffer such a remorse. If, on the one hand, it seems that such a crime is beyond the possibility of human nature, so, on the other hand, granted that a man could be found to commit the crime, it seems that such a criminal ought to be beyond all reach of sorrow or remorse. There is Judas: so vile that he can dip his hand with Christ in the dish and then go out and betray Him; yet so sorry for his crime that he goes out and hangs himself.

Having mentioned in this way the remorse of Judas, I now consider for a moment those analyses of Judas' crime which make it not a crime at all. Undoubtedly, the record of the remorse of Judas has been the fountain whence these theories or explanations have flowed. Since it is difficult to reconcile the remorse of Judas with his transgression, efforts have been made to seek for motives other than those which the Scriptures attribute to Judas, or rather hint at, for it is highly significant that the Gospels merely state that Judas was a traitor, that he betrayed Him, they do not say *why* he betrayed Him.

TRAITOR OR TRICKSTER

Archbishop Whately is prominent among those who elaborated the hypothesis that Judas was not a traitor in the sense that he sought to compass the death of Jesus. The foundation stone of this theory is that Judas, in common with all the disciples, was looking forward to the establishment of a Messianic kingdom by Jesus in which he would have one of the twelve thrones that Jesus had promised to His disciples. He was disappointed that Jesus refused to let the people in Galilee make Him a king (John 6:15), and became more and more impatient as Jesus postponed from day to day the setting up of the Kingdom. Jesus himself had accepted the title of Messiah from the Twelve (Matthew 16:16). Why, then, did He not assume the splendor and take the throne of the Messiah? Judas at length resolves to force such a step on the part of Christ. He plans to precipitate the crisis by bringing Jesus face to face with his adversaries. To accomplish this before the crowds which were attending the Passover had left Jerusalem and dispersed to their own towns and villages, Judas resolves to go through an act of seeming desertion and treason. He will play the part of a traitor and precipitate the crisis between Jesus and those who oppose Him. In that crisis Christ would declare His Messiahship and set up His throne. Judas counted upon forgiveness and restoration and a share in the glory of the kingdom as soon as Jesus understood his action. Because he believed that Jesus was the Messiah he knew He could not die (John 12:34), and even when he had betrayed Him with a kiss in the garden he heard Jesus say that twelve legions of angels were at His command.

But Judas had made a miscalculation. Jesus did acknowledge Himself as the Messiah. Yet, what was unthinkable to Judas, and now filled him with dismay and horror, He permitted Himself to be condemned to death. Judas hurried to the priests and tried to make a last desperate effort to undo the sad matter, and failing in this, overwhelmed with remorse and despair, hanged himself. According to this hypothesis, Judas, for the sake of worldly gain and glory, took great liberties with the person of Jesus, and was led on by consuming avarice, but he was not guilty of willfully contriving the death of Jesus. That is, at heart he was no traitor. In *Discourse on the Treason of Judas Iscariot and Notes,* Archbishop Whately says, "The difference between Iscariot and his fellow-apostles was that, though they all had the same expectations and conjectures, he dared to act on his conjectures, departing from the plain course of his known duty to follow the calculation of his worldly wisdom and the schemes of his worldly ambition."

Thomas De Quincey, in his entertaining essay on Judas, travels over much the same course as that taken by Archbishop Whately, but goes far beyond him. The Archbishop relieved Judas of the odium of treason, of betraying his Friend and Master, but leaves him with the condemnation of colossal covetousness and worldly ambition resting upon him. But De Quincey lifts Judas to the pinnacle of mistaken but sincere and sacrificial zeal for Christ's cause. Here we have a man who willingly takes upon himself the odium and infamy of the traitor, knowing that the Scriptures must be fulfilled, that someone must play the part of a traitor before Jesus asserts His royal powers and takes His throne and reigns. This Judas is no traitor, but the prince of the martyrs. His only mistake was a mistake of judgment, not of love, not of faith, not of avarice. When he saw that he had played the traitor in vain, then his heart broke with remorse and he hanged himself. In De Quincey's own words:

> To burst in the middle is simply to be shattered and ruined in the central organ of our sensibilities, which is the heart; and in saying that the viscera of Iscariot, or his middle, had burst and gushed out, the original reporter meant simply that his heart had broken. That was precisely his case. Out of pure anguish that the schemes which he meant for the sudden glorification of his Master had recoiled (according to all worldly interpretation) in his utter ruin; that the sudden revolution, through a democratic movement, which was to raise himself and his brother apostles into Hebrew princes, had scattered them like sheep without a shepherd; and that, superadded to this common burden of ruin, he personally had to bear a separate load of conscious disobedience to God and insupportable responsibility; naturally enough, out of all this, he fell into fierce despair; his heart broke, and under that storm of affliction he hanged himself.

Unfortunately, this is not the Judas of the Four Gospels. The only source that we have for knowledge that there was a Judas tells us that Judas was a traitor. No scheming politician, hoping to profit by the establishment of the Messianic kingdom, no heroic martyr, taking the part of a traitor in order to fulfill the Scriptures, but one who sold the Son of God for thirty pieces of silver and went to "his own place." The fourth evangelist and St. Luke speak of him and his crime with a shudder, "Satan entered into him."

The first question that we ask about Judas is: How did such a man come to be a member of the Twelve? What place had the son of perdition among the disciples of the Son of Man? That the Scriptures might be fulfilled, that the Son of Man might go as it had been written of Him (Matt. 26:24)? Life has too much deep tragedy in it, too many instances of members of the same apostolic band, the same family, the same class, the objects of the same father's prayers, those who kneeled at the same mother's knee—going some of them to the light, to honor, to faith, hope and love and good works, and some of them to the dark, to shame, to infamy, to violation of the laws of God and of man—going, like Judas, out into the blackest night, alone, forever alone—for anyone to dismiss with a smile what God's Word teaches us about the eternal decrees and purposes of God. This mystery has been touched upon by Oliver Wendell Holmes in his *Two Streams*:

> Behold the rocky wall
> That down its sloping sides
> Pours the swift raindrops, blending as they fall,
> In rushing river-tides!
>
> Yon stream, whose sources run
> Turned by a pebble's edge,
> Is Athahasca, rolling toward the sun
> Through the cleft mountain-ledge.
>
> The slender rill had strayed,
> But for the slanting stone,
> To evening's ocean, with the tangled braid
> Of foam-flecked Oregon.
>
> So from the heights of Will
> Life's parting stream descends,
> And, as a moment turns its slender rill,
> Each widening torrent bends,

> From the same cradle's side,
>   From the same mother's knee,
> One to long darkness and the frozen tide,
>   One to the Peaceful Sea!

In more telling language it has been dealt with by Rossetti in his *Jenny*:

> Just as another woman sleeps!
> Enough to throw one's thoughts in heaps
> Of doubt and horror—what to say
> Or think—this awful secret sway,
> The potter's power over the clay!
> Of the same lump (it has been said)
> For honor and dishonor made,
> Two sister vessels. Here is one.

We can neither add to nor take from the words of Scripture concerning this mystery, and there, in humble awe, knowing that the Judge of all earth must do right, we leave it. But we can speak of Judas on the side of his own will, his own decrees, his own place. We cannot think either that he was chosen to play the part of the traitor as a stage manager might choose an actor to take the villain's part in a play, or that Judas joined the cause of Christ with purposes of treachery in his heart, or even with unworthy mercenary motives. As we have seen, all the disciples hoped to gain something by the surrender they had made to Christ. Christ himself seemed to countenance such hopes. When Peter said, "Lo, we have left all and followed Thee," Jesus responded that His disciples would receive "an hundredfold, now in this time, houses, and brethren, and sisters" (Mark 10:28-30).

WHAT WERE HIS MOTIVES?

Very likely Judas was as sincere in his motives and as worthy or unworthy as the rest of the disciples. He had good in him and evil, but while contact with Christ drew out the good and banished the evil in the other disciples, with Judas the reverse seems to have been the case. With him Christ was a savor of death unto death. Avarice undoubtedly played its part in his downfall. If so, how telling the words of Jesus about laying up treasure in heaven! John says plainly that he was a thief and pilfered from the bag. His thieving instinct made him blow with his tainted breath upon the beautiful offering of Mary to Jesus, complaining that the money might have been given to the poor. But once in the bag, Judas, and not the poor, would have profited by the sum. Leonardo takes him in the moment of the question at the table, "Lord, is it I?" There he sits, furtive-browed and dark-visaged, clutching the bag with an eager right hand.

It has been objected that if avarice were a motive in the crime, Judas should have profited more by continued stealings from the treasury, whereas the act of treachery brought him but twenty dollars and put an end to all further gain. But it is best to be guided here not by what other men might have done under similar circumstances, but by what Judas did. He sold Him for thirty pieces of silver. If avarice played its part in the breakdown of the character of Judas, it is nothing strange or unheard of. Men with visions of the truth and with a supply of good motives have been brought to disastrous ends through love of filthy lucre. Witness the gifted Balaam, who could wish he were of the number of Israel and could die the death of the righteous Hebrews, yet for gold is eager to curse them. Those two men, the admiring, truth-desiring, peace-seeking man, and the other money-loving, good-hating man, resided in the heart of Balaam and in the heart of Judas, and, alas! in the heart of many a man since. For the sake of money, and what money can bring, "just for a piece of silver," men have deserted noble causes and played false that great cause of truth and righteousness which, once at least in every man's life, calls upon him to serve her.

That Judas was shocked at the pretensions of Jesus, at His making Himself co-equal with God, at His fierce denunciations of the ruling classes at Jerusalem, and was actuated by patriotic motives in deserting Jesus, or that he was jealous of the Galilean disciples, he himself being the only Judean, we dismiss as pure imagination and contrary to the record, the only record we have.

There are, however, not wanting evidences that vindictiveness and revenge entered into his crime, as well as avarice. We must try to account for the hate that Judas bore to Jesus leading him to such a step. It is no uncommon experience that the darkness

has the light. Judas knew that Jesus knew from the beginning
that he was a traitor, or had treasonable propensities. Once He
said that one of His disciples had a devil. Judas knew whom He
meant. Jesus warned and reproved him, but these warnings, instead of recalling him and making him repent, sent him farther
along the path of crime. It is significant that both Matthew and
Mark say it was after Jesus had rebuked him for interfering with
Mary's gift of precious ointment that Judas began to seek opportunity to betray Him. The devil of vengeance began to brood in
the heart of Judas.

This helps us to understand the kiss in the Garden. The leaders of the band knew Jesus, it was not necessary that He should
be so identified. But to a vindictive, revenge-seeking spirit, the
darkest, cruelest spirit that can take hold of man or woman, how
sweet that kiss in the Garden! God save us from the soul-de-
stroying monster of sin in the form of hate or vindictiveness.
There is nothing which can so quickly banish the good that is in
the man and summon up all of hell, of Satan, of the devil and his
children that is in us as that spirit. Invite that spirit, and Satan
enters into you!

SURRENDERED TO SATAN?

When Judas had received the sop, two things happened: Jesus
said to him, "That thou doest, do quickly," and Satan entered into
him. The words of Jesus and the receiving of the sop marked the
crisis in the soul of Judas. Now there was no further delaying, no
longer halting between two opinions, no longer playing the part
of a traitor and yet remaining a disciple. The hour had come when
Judas had to choose between good and evil, between Christ and
gold, between the light and darkness. Judas chose the dark, the
night, and immediately Satan, who had entered into him before
only by way of suggestion and temptation, now entered in to
possess his own. Not until a man makes that final decision for evil,
against the good, does Satan enter in to possess him. The words of
Jesus, the last save the exclamation in the Garden that Jesus ever
addressed to Judas, "That thou doest, do quickly!" may be taken as
a last warning, perhaps a last appeal. Which would Judas do,
betray Him or be faithful to Him?

There have been worse men than Judas, for men who have been guilty of sin like his, who at least have done it unto "one of the least of these" and, therefore, unto Christ, have yet not taken it to heart as Judas did. However infamous his sin, let us give Judas credit for a corresponding remorse. "Then Judas, which had betrayed Him, when he saw that He was condemned, repented himself and brought again the thirty pieces of silver to the chief priests and elders, saying, I have sinned, in that I have betrayed the innocent blood!" Now we begin to pity him. Yes, every wrong-doer comes at length to that place where men and angels must pity him, where the wrongdoer himself must pity his ruined self. Judas had sold himself.

> Still as of old,
> Man by himself is priced,
> For thirty pieces Judas sold
> Himself, not Christ.

However we may analyze the motives of Judas, his career and his end dispose effectually of the very popular "moral environment theory," that good surroundings invariably make good men, and that bad men are just the natural result of bad surroundings. None could have had better surroundings than Judas had for three years. He walked and he talked with Christ, with Him who is the Way, the Truth and the Life. Yet look at his end! Ah, in evil there are greater mysteries than the accidents of birth and place and station. The right kind of surroundings will help a man if he in his heart so wills it, but if his heart wills it not, then heaven itself would not keep him from going to destruction. It is possible to be near to Christ, to be in His Church, to sit at His table as Judas did, and yet be far from Him.

The last reference we have to Judas, that of St. Luke in the Acts, tells us that Peter, asking the disciples to choose a successor, said, "He went to his own place." His own! It was what he had fashioned, in spite of the influence of Jesus, in spite of the warnings and the appeals of Jesus. There are probably worse places than the one to which Judas went, for it is not difficult to conceive of worse men than Judas. To say that men go to their "own place" relieves this dark subject of future and everlasting retribution of any question of injustice, of overseverity, but it takes nothing away from its solemnity. His own place! My own place! Your own place! What is it now? What would you like it to be? Invite God's Holy Spirit to help you build the place where you would like to live and reign.

13

MATTHIAS

Man is always in a hurry; God takes His time. Whenever man's soul stirs with a vision of a great enterprise he feels that he must embark upon it at once and that an hour's delay may prove fatal. The greatest enterprise ever undertaken by man, an enterprise upon the success of which depends the earthly and eternal happiness of unborn millions, is about to be launched. Earnest and enthusiastic men, ready to die for it, are anxious to put their hands to the task. But Christ tells them to wait—"Wait for the promise of the Father, which ye have heard from me" (Acts 1:4). Every hour and every day is full of opportunity for preaching the Gospel at Jerusalem and throughout the world. But Christ tells them to wait for the baptism of the Holy Spirit. The first ten days of Christian history were days of waiting.

> Men are impatient, and for precipitating things; but the Author of nature appears deliberate throughout His operations; accomplishing His natural ends by slow, successive steps. The ways of Providence are not confined within narrow limits; He hurries not Himself to display today the consequences of the principles that He yesterday laid down; He will draw it out in the lapse of ages, when the hour is come; and even according to our reasoning, logic is not the less sure because it is slow. Providence is unconcerned as to time (if I may be allowed the use of the simile); His march is like that of the fabulous deities of Homer through space; He takes a step, and ages have elapsed. How long a time, how many events,

103

before the regeneration of the moral man by Christianity exercised its great and legitimate influence upon the regeneration of the social state! It has succeeded, however; who can at this day gainsay it? (Guizot: *Lectures on Civilization*, Lecture I).

A WAITING CHURCH

Those first ten days of waiting were prophetic of the history of the Church. In one sense Church history is the story of noble enterprise, of heroic battles with darkness and wickedness in high and low places, of men dreaming great dreams and struggling to make those dreams come true—Christ preached among the Gentiles, Europe and Africa and Asia and the Americas and the isles of the seas evangelized; of martyrs testifying to their faith in Jesus with their life blood; of innumerable ministers and disciples and churches, all unknown to fortune and to fame, in their day and place and generation striving to declare Jesus Christ unto the world. But in another sense Church history is but the repetition of these first ten days: it is the history of waiting. He who gave them the promise of the Holy Spirit gave them the promise of Himself. However the return of Jesus has been interpreted in past ages, however abused by ignorance and fanaticism, there has always beat within the heart of the Church the hope and expectation of some great thing that God has in store for His Church and the world.

> Mid toil and tribulation
> And tumult of her war,
>   She waits the consummation
> Of peace forever more;
>   Till with the vision glorious
> Her longing eyes are blest,
>   And the great Church victorious
> Shall be the Church at rest.

The ten days between the Ascension of Christ and Pentecost were spent by the apostles in prayer. Their place of meeting was the "upper chamber," very likely that very chamber where Jesus sat with them at the Last Supper. In addition to the eleven apostles there were the female adherents of Christ and His relatives. Luke says that at the time of the election of Matthias there were one hundred and twenty gathered together. It was then that Peter, whose place of leadership seems to have been taken for granted by the rest, despite his denial of Christ, stood up and recommended that they choose a successor to Judas, "who went to his own place." Pascal has noted as one of the superior marks of the New Testament that it is free from abuse and vituperation towards those who compassed the death of Jesus. Here we have an instance of this in Peter's remarks concerning Judas. He says plainly that Judas had a part in their ministry, that he was one of the Twelve, but that he had fallen away and gone to his own place.

We can discern almost a note of tenderness in Peter's comment on the apostate disciple. Perhaps he was thinking how nearly he himself had gone in the same direction, and how it was only by the grace of God that he still had his place among the apostles. The falling away of Judas must be made good by the election of a successor. This action Peter justifies from his reading of Psalms 69 and 109. He then proceeds to state the qualifications for membership in the band of the apostles. "Of the men, therefore, that have companioned with us all the time that the Lord Jesus went in and went out among us, beginning from the baptism of John, unto the day that He was received up from us, of these must one become a witness with us of His resurrection" (Acts 1:21,22).

This statement is very significant, first, as to the chief business of the apostles. They were to be witnesses for Christ and the great fact that they had to tell about Him, the fact upon which they based all else, was the fact of His resurrection from the dead. If a man could not testify that Jesus had risen from the dead, if he did not believe that with his whole heart and strength and mind, he had, in the opinion of Peter, no right to speak for Christ to the world, and for the simple reason that he had nothing to tell. For the office of the ministry the candidate must be no novice, but yesterday converted and brought into the Church, but one who had been with Jesus and with the disciples from the very beginning of the ministry of Christ. He was one who had gone in and out among them, that is, one whose character they knew and did not have to take upon the say-so of others.

Men suddenly reclaimed from lives of sin, with their hearts on fire for God, have done mighty works for Him before others, and these works, because thus done, have attracted the notice of the world. But the far greater work has been done by men like Justus and Matthias who came into the ministry with a Christian history and Christian tradition back of them, fathers before them, it may be, who stood in the same office, mothers and grandmothers in whom the light of faith had brightly shone.

There were two men whom all this company agreed to have the qualifications enumerated by Peter, and by unanimous consent these two men, Justus and Matthias, were put forward. Of neither of them have we heard a single word before, of neither of them shall we hear again. But there they were, disciples of Jesus, faithful and honorable men, taking the burdens of faith upon them, and in their day and in the pages of history consigned to obscurity, caring only for the praise of God and not for the praise of men. Who is this Justus? Who is this Matthias? we ask. What right have these nobodies to stand for the high office of the apostolate? They had the right of faith and character and fidelity. Ordinarily, in political affairs today, one of the qualifications for a candidate with the people is that they should have heard much about him. But for every candidate of whom we have heard much there are thousands upon thousands of whom we have heard nothing, who are just as well, perhaps better, qualified to hold the office in question.

If they had been holding their election today, the company of disciples probably would have voted as we do at our meetings. But the method then in vogue, the method of the Old Testament, was to select by lot, and therefore by lot they elected. Their procedure is full of suggestion for us in the choices and decisions that we must make in our life: first, all that your own judgment and wisdom, your experience and conscience can suggest and approve, then, the guidance of God. Neither of these men, so far as the others could tell, would have been unworthy of the apostolate, but only one could be chosen and in some way they had to choose that one.

You may have reduced the possible courses open to you to two; that is, you have refused anything that savors of unbelief or dishonor, and yet be in a dilemma as to which of the two to take. Life demands some sort of a decision. It is your part to choose—for a lot was, after all, a human manipulation—just as these disciples did, and ask God's blessing upon the choice. In connection with this bit of Church history, it is interesting to note that certain Christian sects who follow the torch of the literalist have adhered to this form of electing their ministers.

The lot fell on Matthias. Therefore one cannot but think of Justus. His name probably was no misnomer: he was a good man and a just—so far as the disciples could tell, as good and just and worthy as Matthias. But the lot fell on Matthias. The man upon whom the lot did not fall provokes a train of thought not less than that man upon the lot fell. In the Book of the Kings we read that Tibni died and Omri reigned. There could not be two kings at the same time; there could not be two successors chosen for the place of Judas, but only one. How much of life is the history of how the lot has missed one man and fallen upon another! There is one office, but only one candidate will be elected; one race, but only one will win the prize. "Know ye not that they which run in a race run all, but one receiveth the prize?" (1 Cor. 9:24).

I have sometimes thought, watching some of the collegiate athletic meets and seeing the defeated and conquered runners coming wearily to the tape far behind the victor who has been acclaimed by the multitude, how there could be no glory and no cheers for the victor were it not for the beaten and vanquished runners who come toiling after him. And this is like the race of life—two candidates, but one number that decides who shall be elected. I doubt not that Justus was worthy of his name and was the first to step forward and congratulate Matthias, the successful candidate. He and all the disciples had prayed, had asked God to show of these two the one whom He had chosen, and underneath the incident of the lot they trusted in the overruling Providence of God. For us much of the sting of bitterness, the sorrow of defeat, the thought of what might have been is removed and assuaged when we do what duty commands and let God make the appointments that He wills. "The lot is cast into the lap, but the whole disposing thereof is of the Lord" (Prov. 16:33).

MEET MATTHIAS

Sin had broken the apostolic circle; the number appointed by Christ had been reduced to eleven. The first act of Church history

is the election of Matthias. In him, therefore, I find an emblem of
the perfection of the Church. Always, as we survey it, the Church
is incomplete, imperfect, the wheat and the tares growing together, the good and bad fishes in the same net. But that is not the
final state of the Church. The havoc wrought by sin will be undone; the place of the son of perdition will be taken by the son of
prayer. Christ loves the Church and died for it, and not in vain but
"that He might sanctify it, having cleansed it by the washing of
water with the word, that He might present the Church to Himself a glorious Church, not having spot or wrinkle or any such
thing; but that it should be holy and without blemish" (Eph.
5:26,27). Ever across the clouds and tear-wet vista of the Christian
there extends the glorious rainbow of perfection, not a single
color, not a single grace, not a single virtue lacking.

And when we speak of the Church and the perfection of the
Church we mean a perfection that takes place in the members of
the Church, the true followers of and believers in Christ. Even for
the best and noblest of the saints sin has marred the perfection of
life: we cannot do all that we would do here; time and fading
strength close down many avenues of adventure for the yearning
spirit; love finds its companion and then wakes from dreams of
happiness to find that misfortune or death has taken that companion from it. In our best moments we feel that we should like to
live forever, that we ought to live forever; but alas! death parts us
from our hopes and our ambitions. But Christ is the symbol of the
soul's perfection, of the soul's immortality. On earth we do groan,
longing to be clothed upon, there we shall be clothed upon: here
the Father's word as to the inheritance, there the possession in full
of the inheritance incorruptible, undefiled and that fadeth not
away.

> The One remains, the many change and pass;
> Heaven's light forever shines, Earth's shadows fly;
> Life, like a dome of many colored glass,
> Stains the white radiance of Eternity,
> Until Death tramples it to fragments—Die,
> If thou wouldst be with that which thou dost seek!

14

JAMES, THE LORD'S BROTHER

I have now concluded the sketches of the twelve men who were
members of the original apostolic circle as constituted by Jesus,
and of Matthias, who was chosen by the disciples to take the place
of Judas. But, as our subject involves a consideration of the sources
of Christian history and is a study of the lives of the men who,
acting at those sources, were mighty agents of destiny, it will be
altogether apposite that we should consider two other men, who,
although not of the original twelve, took a great part in the
dissemination of Christianity—first, James, the brother of the Lord
and the head of the Church at Jerusalem, and in a subsequent
chapter, Paul, the Apostle to the Gentiles.

When Peter had been delivered by the angel out of the prison
of Herod and had at last been admitted into the room where some
of the disciples were met together in prayer, he rehearsed to the
amazed and half incredulous gathering what had befallen him, and
then said, "Tell these things unto James and to the brethren."
Peter wanted James to know. James was the most important per-
sonage in the Church at Jerusalem, and it was natural that Peter
should have desired him to know of the wonderful deliverance.

Wherever James appears in the book of the Acts it is in that
relationship, James and the Brethren. When Paul went up to Jerusalem to confer with the leaders there about the Gentile Christians,
it is James who speaks as having authority; and again, when Paul
made his last visit to Jerusalem, Luke says, "Paul went in with us
unto James, and all the elders were present" (Acts 21:18). In his

letter to the Galatians (2:9), Paul names James together with Peter and John as a pillar of the Church, and he names James first, "James and Peter and John, they who were reputed to be pillars, gave to me and Barnabas the right hand of fellowship, that we should go unto the Gentiles." There is no doubt, then, about the place which James the brother of the Lord occupied in the early Church.

AN EQUAL APOSTLE

Was he also an apostle? Not that he was one of the Twelve, but in the sense that Paul was an apostle, commissioned by God to teach and preach with apostolic authority? Of this we may not be sure. In his letter to the Galatians, Paul tells of his first visit to Jerusalem and how he spent fifteen days with Peter, and then adds, "But other of the apostles saw I none, save James the Lord's brother" (Gal. 1:19). A very natural interpretation is that Paul refers to James as an apostle of equal standing with Peter. But whether he does or not, it is clear that he regarded James as a person of authority and influence in no way inferior to that of Peter himself. Peter, too, recognizes the hegemony of James, for, when he has been delivered from the sword of Herod, his first request is that James be informed of what has transpired.

In our study of James the son of Alphaeus, or James the Less, we saw how James the brother of the Lord has often been identified with James the son of Alphaeus, and one of the chief reasons for such identification was the fact that, according to one reading, Paul calls James the Lord's brother and an apostle. But we know of just two men who were apostles and bore the name of James, one the son of Zebedee and the other the son of Alphaeus. Therefore, the apostle who was the Lord's brother must be the apostle who was the son of Alphaeus. But the argument is inconclusive and creates greater difficulties than it solves. If James the son of Alphaeus is James the brother of the Lord, what shall we do with their fathers? If James is the brother of the Lord, then his father was Joseph and not Alphaeus. The difficulty, as I have indicated in the study of James the Less, is gotten around by saying that James was a brother of the Lord in the sense that he was a cousin, probably the son of Mary, a sister of Mary the mother of Jesus and the wife of Cleophas. But this would leave two sisters with the same name, Mary, and would make the word *adelphos*, brother, mean only a relative, and not, as it always does except in the new Christian sense of brothers in Christ, a uterine brother in the flesh.

One of the chief reasons why this identification of James the Lord's brother with James the son of Alphaeus has been so eagerly sought is the teaching of the Roman Church on the perpetual virginity of Mary. To those who indulge in Mariolatry it has seemed a thing abhorrent that, after having been the mother of Jesus by the Holy Spirit, Mary should have borne children to her husband Joseph. Even a reverence of Mary which falls far short of Mariolatry might be tempted to wish Mary was forever a virgin. But, upon second thought, if Christ was to humble Himself to be born of a virgin, why should He have hesitated to have brothers in the flesh? Or, if Mary as a virgin was the mother of Jesus, how could she be defiled by bearing other children to her husband, an office of which men have always conceived as an exaltation of womanhood? Others who do not hold to the perpetual virginity of Mary like to think that these brothers were sons of Joseph by a former marriage. Such, at least, they must have been, and, from the plain reading of the Gospels, sons of the same mother.

FOUR BROTHERS

There were four of these brothers of Jesus—James, Joseph, Simon and Judas. When Jesus had been teaching in the synagogue at Nazareth his townsfolk, though unwilling to believe on Him, had to admit the penetration of His teaching, for they said: "Whence hath this man this wisdom and these mighty works? Is not this the carpenter's son? Is not His mother called Mary, and His brethren James, and Joseph, and Simon, and Judas? and His sisters, are they not all with us? When then hath this Man all these things?" (Matt. 13:54-56). Because James is mentioned first he was probably the eldest of the four.

Dr. Alexander Whyte in his study of James says what I believe is true of us all when he writes: "I often imagine myself to be James. I far oftener imagine myself to be in James' place and experience than in the place and experience of any other man in the whole Bible or the whole world. The first thirty years of James' life fascinate me and enthrall me far more than all the rest of human life and human history taken together. And I feel sure that I am not alone in that fascination of mine. Who, indeed, would not be absolutely captivated, fascinated and enthralled, both in imagination and in heart, at the thought of holding James' relationship to Jesus Christ!" What he means is that when we think of Jesus before the days of His public ministry we wonder how He acted, what He said, and what relationship He bore to His parents and to His brothers and His sisters.

Jesus was the eldest son in this large family. As such He and James, the next eldest, would have a natural fellowship and relationship. I remember in my own family how the two eldest brothers formed a group of themselves, in sports, interests, studies, and how the two youngest formed a second group. James, then, would be in the company of this first-born brother, Jesus. Here imagination may paint its scenes of interest and possibility, and probability, too, while history is mute.

Did James and Jesus toil together in the carpenter's shop? Together did they trudge after their mother as she went to the village well to draw water? Together did they follow with eager boyish steps and bursting wonder and admiration, or fear, perhaps, the band of Roman legionnaires who one day strode haughtily through their town? Did they, now a little older, take an excursion to the famous plain of Esdraelon, just south of the valley in which Nazareth stood on its little declivity, where some of the great battles in the history of Israel had been fought? Did they ever go with their father to Tiberias and look with wonder on the Sea of Galilee, experiencing that thrill which every inland boy has felt when first he looks at the sea and beholds the flapping of a sail? Did they repeat together to their mother or their father verses from the Psalms or the prophets? Did James ever get angry with Jesus? Did Jesus and James act as nurse for some of the younger children, and was it then that Jesus learned how to deal with children, so that when afterwards He wished to illustrate a sermon with a child it was the easiest and most natural thing in the world for Him to take a little child up into His arms? These, and a hundred other questions come thronging upon the mind the moment we launch out upon this sea of imagination.

JAMES AND JESUS

What we actually do know of the relationship between Jesus and His brothers during the days of His ministry is sad and not altogether to the credit of James and the other three. "Even His brethren did not believe on Him" is the record of John 7:5. When the people in Galilee were getting ready to go to Jerusalem to the feast of the tabernacles, and Jesus chose to remain in Galilee, His brethren came to Him and said: "Depart hence, and go into Judea, that Thy disciples also may behold Thy works which Thou doest. For no man doeth anything in secret, and himself seeketh to be known openly. If Thou doest these things, manifest Thyself unto the world. For even His brethren did not believe on Him. Jesus therefore saith unto them, My time is not yet come; but your time is always ready. The world cannot hate you; but Me it hateth, because I testify of it, that its works are evil. Go ye up unto the feast. I go not up unto this feast, because My time is not yet fulfilled. And having said these things unto them, He abode still in Galilee" (John 7:3-9).

What we have here is what Jesus often encountered in the Twelve themselves, a total misapprehension of the spiritual nature of His Kingdom. James and the other brothers wanted Christ to center His work at Jerusalem. He said He was the Messiah: then let Him take the Messiah's place and the Messiah's city. It was an irritating and impertinent interference and merited a more severe answer than Jesus in His calm patience made them. It was the spirit, not of unbelief altogether, but of misunderstanding and arrogant proprietorship in Christ and His plans because He was their brother in the flesh. Upon another occasion, when He had been preaching in the synagogue at Capernaum, He was interrupted by a messenger from His relatives, who said to Him, "Behold, Thy mother and Thy brethren stand without, seeking to speak to Thee. But He answered and said unto him that told Him, Who is My mother? and who are My brethren? And He stretched forth His hand toward His disciples, and said, Behold My mother and My brethren! For whosoever shall do the will of My Father who is in heaven, he is My brother, and sister, and mother!" (Matt. 12:47-50).

His rebuke strikes us as very severe, especially when we are

accustomed to press upon men and women the sacred importance
of the relationships and obligations of the home. But Jesus had
spoken the truth. The twelve disciples, with all their faults, were
nearer to Christ than His brothers in the flesh, for Him they
better understood and loved. St. Mark records for us another
instance of the officiousness and misapprehension of the brethren
of Jesus. After Jesus had ordained the Twelve and sent them forth,
"they went into an house. And the multitude cometh together
again, so that they could not so much as eat bread. And when His
friends heard of it, they went out to lay hold on Him; for they
said, He is beside Himself" (Mark 3:19-21). No doubt these
"friends" included the "brethren" of the Lord. It must have wound-
ed Him far more than that which we read in the following verses
was said of Him by the scribes, that is, that He had Beelzebub and
by him cast out devils.

There is a suggestion also of jealousy in the impatience of His
brethren and their readiness to declare Him demented. But we
must give them credit for this, that they never put themselves
altogether beyond the reach of the influence of Jesus; they said
things that hurt Him and refused to affirm their belief in Him, but
when He was crucified they ("all His acquaintance," Luke 23:49)
stood afar off beholding. After the resurrection they are mentioned as being present in the upper chamber, engaged in prayer
and worship with the disciples and the women.

His Family Rejected Him

Yet, during the years when Christ needed most of all their
sympathy and help, they were indifferent or impudent and arrogant. Truly, He trod the winepress alone, and to His own people
He looked and there was none to help. That touching phrase, "He
came unto His own, and His own received Him not" (John 1:11)
takes on a deeper pathos when we remember that not only His
own nation but His own family did not receive Him. We wonder
why this was. Perhaps it was to show us that flesh and blood
cannot inherit the Kingdom of God, but that a man must be born
of the Spirit into the rare friendship and fellowship of Christ.
Certainly, upon no other grounds can one account for the different attitude taken toward Jesus by men of the same environment,

the same family, the same church. Perhaps, too, these men suffered and were handicapped by their very proximity to Jesus. Not that familiarity with Him could breed contempt, or that there was aught in the life of Jesus, that hidden life of thirty years, which was inconsistent with His three years of public ministry, but the fact that He had lived under their roof, eaten of their bread, joined in their labor, made it the more difficult for them to see in Him the world's Redeemer and the One altogether lovely.

Men who have crossed the seas to visit some shrine of religion, or art, or liberty, have been amazed to find men living hard by it utterly indifferent to it, or totally ignorant of it. It is not always the peasant sickling his hay and milking his goats on the mountains of Norway who sees the sublime beauty of the deep, silent fjords and the cascades that hurl themselves with deep and never-ceasing antiphonals down the steep mountainsides. Hawthorne's legend of the Great Stone Face finds its fulfillment in daily life. The Epistle to the Hebrews speaks of entertaining angels unawares. This is the common experience of life. After they are gone, faded away on the horizon of life's flat desert, and we are left standing like Abraham beneath the quiet oaks of meditation and reflection, then, but with a conscience not so good as that of Abraham, we perceive that angels have passed our way. The earthen vessel stands unhonored and unappreciated in our homes; but one day death lifts its grim mallet and breaks the vase, and we find that it was an alabaster box of ointment, precious, very costly. We carry our burdens and trudge our dusty roads to the Emmaus of our desires and purposes, and never know that he who has companied with us by the way was one who would have been welcomed in the elect company of the sons of God.

> Be merciful, O our God!
>> Forgive the meanness of our human hearts,
>> That never, till a noble soul departs,
>> See half the worth, or hear the angel's wings
>> Till they go rustling heavenward as he springs
> Up from the mounded sod.

As between Peter of the denial and Peter of the Day of Pentecost there stands one great fact, a special appearance of the Lord, so between the James who did not believe in Jesus and the James who leads the Church at Jerusalem and who, in all probability commences the letter that bears his name by describing himself as "James, the slave of the Lord Jesus Christ," there stands one great fact, the appearance unto him of the Lord. St. Paul it is who tells us of this appearance, "He was seen of James" (1 Cor. 15:7). James was won to Christ, changed from a doubter, a ridiculer, to a slave of Christ by that special appearance. Peter, James and Paul, all had this peculiar blessing and great opportunity. This appearance would itself exalt James to apostolic rank. Here, too, as in the case of Peter, imagination would like to wander. The special appearance and, let it be remembered, the first appearance, to Mary Magdalene was an appearance to comfort and console the broken heart that loved Him; the special appearance to Peter was an appearance to a disciple who loved Him and believed in Him, but who had been tempted by Satan to deny Him; the special appearance to Paul, one born out of due time, was an appearance to a man who was making it the business of his life to oppose Christianity and persecute it from the face of the earth. The special appearance to James was to a man who never openly opposed Christ, or persecuted Him, and yet, although he had been much with Him, had never surrendered his mind and heart to the dominion of Christ. Christ had been a long time with James, but James had not known Him. But at length, changed by the appearance of the Lord, he came to love Him and to trust Him. The skeptic and the self-willed became the "slave."

I speak to men and women who have been much with Christ. You have heard of Him and His works from earliest childhood, and His sayings are familiar to your ears. I will not say that you have not loved Him and followed Him, for you have, far longer, perhaps, than have I. But as you think upon this theme of your relationship to Christ, is it not true that of certain areas of your character, of certain periods of life, you, too, must say, "I did not believe on Him; I did not even see Him, for between me and Him there was a thick cloud of my own desires and my own stubborn pride"? If so, ask Him to reveal Himself anew to you, letting you behold His beauty, so that, caught and charmed by His loveliness, you will desire like James to become His slave.

It may chance that some of those who shall read these pages

may be like James who has not hitherto believed in Jesus, although perfectly familiar with the Church and the Bible and all the reasons for believing on Christ. But the days, yes, the years have slipped by and still you do not believe and confess. The experience of James is your hope. He was a child of the evening, a late blooming in the autumn. The fact that Christ appeared unto James lets you know that He wants you, too, to become His friend, His disciple, His slave.

15

PAUL

O n a March afternoon in the year of salvation 60 A.D., a gang of prisoners under the custody of a Roman centurion is descending the western slope of the Alban Hills. Each prisoner is chained to a soldier. This one is a man-stealer from Alexandria, this one a robber from Tyre, this one a murderer from Caesarea, this one a rebel from Jerusalem. All look the part save this last prisoner, who is a Hebrew who has appealed to the jurisdiction of Caesar, and is being taken to Rome to stand before Caesar's judgment seat.

The Appian Way leads them across the vast spaces of the Roman campaign, now brilliant with the flowers of springtime. Now they are passing over the plain which, at a day not far distant, will be honeycombed with narrow subterranean passages, where men will lay their dead in hope of the doctrine of the resurrection which fell from the lips of the Jewish prisoner. As they come nearer to the city, the road is filled with throngs of people, coming and going— farmers returning with empty carts from the market, cohorts of soldiers starting for the distant east or coming home after service in Africa, Greece or Asia, wealthy men carried in litters by slaves on their way to their summer villas on the hills, the chariots of generals and senators and proconsuls.

To Julius and his band of prisoners all these give hardly a glance as they pass. Now the prisoners pass by the colossal tombs of the great men of Rome, then at length into the city, past temples, statues, arches, baths, colonnades and places, whose gilded roofs flash back the afternoon sundown into the Forum and up the Capitoline Hill to the barracks of the Praetorian Guard, where Julius hands over his prisoners.

The dream of one of these prisoners has come true! He has come to Rome! Yet, save among a few obscure believers, his entry excited not a ripple of interest or comment. Rome's greatest conqueror entered her gates that day. When the proud monuments of imperial splendor upon which this prisoner gazed as he passed through the city shall have been leveled with the dust and under the dust, Rome's most conspicuous monument will be a temple dedicated to the faith of that lonely prisoner.

It is not my purpose to speak of Paul's place in history. That place is forever secure. As one of the inspired texts of history, St. Paul needs no explanation and no defense. What I wish to do rather is to say something of the man who did these mighty works, the messenger who carried the message which turned the world upside down, the lamp which bore the light which lighted the darkness of this world.

Paul once asked the Corinthians to be followers of him as he was of Christ. Who could imitate Paul, the versatility of his genius, his great experience with Christ, the power and cogency of his thought and the eloquence of his tongue? Yet there is much in him which is capable of imitation and where humble Christians can follow him. Of that let us now speak.

HIS SELF-IMAGE

First, his appreciation of the dignity of human nature. This is always a mark of a great soul. Paul showed his high thought of the worth and dignity of man by a high regard for himself. I have always counted it a fortunate thing that he who is the great teacher as to the sinfulness of man and the corruption of human nature was no mealy-mouthed weakling, but the manliest man who ever lived. We have an instance of this in Paul's reply to the Roman officers at Philippi, who, when they discovered that they had scourged and imprisoned without trial a Roman citizen, sent down messengers asking Paul to withdraw quietly from the city. But Paul answered in all the splendor of his self-respect, "They have beaten us openly, uncondemned, being Romans, and they cast us into prison: and now do they thrust us out privily? Nay, verily: but let them come themselves and fetch us out." We have another echo of this in his rebuke of the high priest who, at the trial of Paul before the Sanhedrin, commanded the soldier to smite Paul on the mouth. Instantly Paul scorched him with the flame of his righteous indignation: "God shall smite thee, thou whited wall, for sittest thou to judge me after the law and commandest me to be smitten contrary to the law?" It was a ringing testimony to the rights of man. Paul was able to respect himself because, he tells us, he always lived so as to have a conscience void of offense toward God and man. If Paul was a chosen vessel, let it be remembered that he was also a clean vessel before he was chosen. The first factor in any good and useful life is the respect of self. The man who does not live so as to have his own self-respect cannot hope to reach or touch other men.

> Self-knowledge, self-reverence, self-control—
> These three alone lead life to sovereign power.

A MAN FOR ALL

Second, his love for others. He who had such high thoughts of the worth and dignity of human nature was a fit vessel to bear to the world the doctrines of the Gospel which affirmed the worth of every soul and a noble destiny through faith in Christ. Yet this love for others was not a natural gift with Paul. Of all men, at the outset, he would seem the least qualified to become the bearer of the tidings that God had made of one blood all nations of men. He appears in the theater of human action as a man possessed by the fiercest prejudices and antipathies, as an intense nationalist of the straitest sect, seeing nothing good beyond the confines of Israel. Yet this man, through the touch of Christ, becomes the apostle to the Gentiles, the first preacher of the doctrine of a nation of humanity, which is above all other nations. His traveling band, made up of Timothy, half Greek and Hebrew, Luke the Greek, Aristarchus and Sopater who were Macedonians, and Trophimus who was an Asiatic, was the first society of internationalists the world had ever seen.

When Paul died, his arms were stretched as wide apart as those of Christ upon the cross. In Chrysostom's eloquent words, "The dust of that heart which a man would not do wrong to call the heart of the world, so enlarged that it could take in cities, and nations, and peoples." The "desperate tides" of the whole world's anguish was forced through the channels of a single heart. "Who is weak and I am not weak? Who is made to stumble and I burn not?" He was debtor to all men, all races, all classes, all colors. Wherever a man breathed, wherever a heart beat, wherever a soul was enshrined, there was Paul with all his burning earnestness and yearning love.

He was able to think nothing alien to himself. When John Howard, the prisoner-reformer, died in a Russian lazzaretto, they put on his grave these words: "Reader, whosoever thou art, know that thou standest by the grave of a friend." Did we know where rests the dust of Paul, we could write like words over his tomb: "Reader, whosoever thou art, bond or free, Greek or barbarian, Jew or Gentile, black or white, red or yellow, man of the first, fifteenth or twentieth century, know that thou standest by the grave of a friend."

A MAN BORN FOR ADVERSITY

Third, the heroic element in the life of Paul. In our day there is a tendency to think that the heroism of the Christian life is to be found apart from great Christian beliefs and convictions. It is, therefore, a fact worthy of pause and reflection that it is the man of the deepest and most clearly outlined beliefs and doctrines who is also the noblest of the Christian heroes, as Chrysostom called him, "the wrestler for Christ."

In his libelous *Life of St. Paul*, Renan, meaning to contrast Paul unfavorably with Jesus, says: "To appear for a moment, to reflect a soft and profound refulgence, to die very young, is the life of a God. To struggle, dispute and conquer is the life of a man." Not in the disparaging sense in which Renan meant it, to struggle, dispute and, sometimes, to conquer, is the life of a man. We do not know a man until we have seen how he performs on the lonely platform of adversity, how he will act with the wind in his face. If there was ever a man born for adversity, and who inspires his fellow-men to take arms against a sea of troubles and by opposing end them, that man was St. Paul. It was no rhetoric, no mere figure of speech, when he spoke of bearing in his body the marks of the Lord Jesus Christ.

What a catalogue of woes he mentions—thorns in the flesh and sicknesses of the body, through adversaries of the civil government, beatings and imprisonment; the frenzy of the mobs, who stoned him and clamored for his blood; the oath-bound assassins who dogged his tracks; the perils of the natural world, by sea, by river, in wilderness and on mountaintop; the desertion and suspicion of his friends and cruel slander which, like a viper, has rustled in the withered leaves of dry and fallen hearts since the world began.

Heroic battler, noble wrestler for Christ! How many were your adversaries! Was there a peril of sky or earth or sea that he did not face? Was there a wicked passion in the heart of man which did not select him for its victim? Was there a cup of bitterness which he did not taste? Was there a thorn to which the flesh is heir that he did not endure? Yet in all things he was more than conqueror.

It is here that all of us become deeply interested in Paul. We all must face life, and, if it can be done triumphantly, we want to know how. In Paul's triumph there were at least three elements:

1. *His aim and purposes did not end with self.* If his own pleasure and comfort and personal success had been his aim, then what a bitter disappointment life must have been to Paul! But he had scorn for those miserable aims which end with self. Personal defeats and overthrows did not shake his soul. Those personal vicissitudes which shock and overcome so many men were but minor incidents to this man, whose mind was set on a higher goal than self.

2. *God had a purpose to work out in his life.* Whatever, therefore, the hard experience through which he had to pass, he could look under it and beyond it and back of it to the will and purpose of God. Things did not "happen" to Paul. The man who gives us the sublime and difficult doctrine about the sovereign decree of Almighty God, is also the man who gives us the incomparable demonstration of how that faith works in everyday life. He not only said it, but found it to be true, that sentence imbedded like a lovely crystal in the dark rock of the great chapter on predestination, "All things work together for good to them that love God."

3. *His fellowship with Christ* was so close that he could make bold to say that Christ suffered in him. Scotland has given many martyrs to the Church and to civil liberty, but there is no tale of martyrdom which so touches a Scottish heart as that of the two Wigtown martyrs, Mary and Agnes Wilson, who perished in the Solway tide. The elder sister was fastened to a stake much farther out than the younger, with the thought that when the younger saw the sufferings and death struggles of her sister she would recant. Quickly the inexorable tide of the Solway came in, first to the ankles, then to the knees, then to the waist, then to the neck, then to the lips. The executioners called to the younger sister, "Look! What seest thou?" Turning her head a little she saw the struggles of her drowning sister, and then made her calm answer, "What do I see? I see the Lord Jesus suffering in one of His members!" In the darkest and most critical hours of his life St. Paul was conscious of the presence and the help of Christ—"But the Lord stood by me."

4. *The friendships of St. Paul.* His was a heart which burned for everyone who was lost and was broken down by a brother's tears. Even if we did not have so many recorded instances of the deeply affectionate nature of St. Paul, we should know him to be that sort of man, for back of every great and good and lasting work there beats somewhere a warm and tender heart. Napoleon at St. Helena wondered if in all the world a single person loved him. But to do justice to the friendships of St. Paul would require the tongue, not of man, but of an angel. In his letters come first the doctrines, then the practical precepts, and last the personal greetings to Onesiphorus, who was not ashamed of his chains; to Epaphroditus, who came to minister to him in Rome and whom Paul nursed back to life; to Amplias, Narcissus, Herodian, Julia, Olympas, Rufus and "his mother and mine"; and then that last urgent message for best loved Timothy to come "before winter."

He who could smite with a Titan's fist the stronghold of Satan knew also how to lay a forget-me-not on the breast of a living friend or upon the grave of the dead. The thought of those friends whom he had made for himself and for Christ, "hearts he had won of sister or of brother, friends in the blameless family of God," the thought of these friends, the remembrance that they prayed for him, came like gleams of sunlight into the damp and gloom of that Mamertine dungeon at Rome. Salute! Salute! Salute! is his word as they lead him out to die. And thus with messages for those whose names he had written in the Lamb's Book of Life, Paul fades from this world into that other world where friends meet and forever are fair and where partings are no more.

All these friendships were summed up in the great and eternal friendship with Christ. That is why Paul's life is the greatest love story ever written. Love carried him over the blazing plains and miasmic marshes; love led him through the ghettos of the great Roman cities; love was the star by which he steered his course through the stormy Agean and Mediterranean. If I were asked to sum up his theology, his doctrine, I would not mention his great fundamental teachings as to the fall of man and the sinfulness that requires redemption; nor his profound statement as to the sovereign purposes of God's grace; nor his logical setting forth of the doctrine of justification by faith. I would sum it up in one single sentence, that sentence which must sum up all genuine Christianity, all true saving relationship with Christ: "I live by the faith of the Son of God, who loved me and gave Himself for me." That mighty life is but the echo of that sentence which takes in the length and the depth and the breadth and the height of our faith, "He loved me and gave Himself for me." Forever true! As true of you as it was of Paul, or John. Christ loved you and gave Himself for you. But have you consented to that fact? Have you bowed down before it? Can you say it as Paul said it, "He loved me and gave Himself for me"?

> Christ! I am Christ's, and let the name suffice you,
>   Yea, for me too He greatly hath sufficed;
> Lo, with no winning word I would entice you,
>   Paul has no honor and no friend but Christ!

16

JOHN THE BAPTIST—
THE FRIEND OF THE BRIDEGROOM [1]

Once on a bright June day I stood upon a summit of the Blue Ridge Mountains. To the north and to the south stretched the mountains, their mighty shoulders draped with a haze of infinite blue. In front of me lay the Cumberland Valley, well watered, like the Garden of the Lord. I could see the fields and orchards with their alternate hues like checkered squares; the white ribbons which marked the fine highways along which a century ago might have been seen the eager soldiery of Lee as his army marched into Pennsylvania; the enormous red barns, the white towers of the hamlet churches, the graystone farmhouses, and man going forth to his labor until the evening. I had often passed through that valley, but it was only when I stood upon the summit of the mountain that I was able to see it in all its length and breadth.

There are times when it is good for us to get above the smoke and dust and confusion of our everyday existence and look at life from some great eminence, where the winds blow fresh and clear and the view is unobstructed. And what better place to stand than upon the shoulders of one of God's great men?

---

1. A sketch of John the Baptist has a legitimate place in a study of the Twelve Apostles, for some of them were disciples of John before they became disciples of Jesus, and all of them, directly or indirectly, were influenced by that mighty personality.

In his life of Thomas Carlyle, John Nicholl quotes a saying of Hegel that "a great man condemns the world to the task of explaining him." In the case of John the Baptist such condemnation is neither unpleasant nor unprofitable. John's brief and fiery ministry of judgment and repentance had come to a close. Because of his fearless denunciation of Herod and Herodias for their adulterous union, John had been cast into prison. There in the lonely dungeon of Machaerius, on the shore of the Dead Sea, John's mighty spirit began to flag and his eagle eye began to film with doubt.

"Art Thou He that should come, or look we for another?" That was the question John sent to Jesus from the dungeon. The answer of Christ was marked by that deep respect with which He always referred to His great forerunner: "Go and show John again those things ye do see: that the blind see, the lame walk, the deaf hear, the broken-hearted are healed, the lepers cleansed, the dead are raised up, and the poor have the Gospel preached to them: and blessed is he whosoever shall not be offended in Me."

That was for John. This world flatters a man to his face and disparages him when his back is turned. Not so Christ. He did not tell John that he was the greatest man that ever lived, but when the messengers of John had gone their way, Jesus turned to the crowd who stood about and who had overheard the conversation and perhaps now doubted that John was a prophet, and said to them: "But what went ye out for to see? A reed shaken with the wind?" A man answering every wind of popular opinion like one of the reeds in the Jordan Valley bending before the vagrant wind? "A man clothed in soft raiment," or looking for a soft place? "But what went ye out to see? A prophet? Yea, and more than a prophet, for I say unto you, among them that are born of women there hath not arisen a greater than John the Baptist." If praise is to be measured by the lips which pronounce it, then never was man so praised as was John the Baptist. In speaking, then, about the greatness of John we shall think, first, of the origin of his greatness, whence it came, and, second, of the content of his greatness, what it was.

THE ORIGIN OF HIS GREATNESS

Let us trace this great river back to its source. The other John, writing of the Baptist, said, "There was a man sent from God, whose name was John." That was as far as John could go in accounting for the greatness of the Baptist. It is as far as any man can go, for over the unfathomed depths of great personality there broods a mystery like that which hovers over the face of the sleeping ocean. Back of all our histories and biographies and heredity and environment and education lies the mighty purpose of God. When the world needs its great soul, God has him in reserve and there is a man sent from God.

But in sending such men into the world, God lets them come through channels and instrumentalities which lie within our observation. I was reading, some time ago, the life of a distinguished American soldier, Albert Sidney Johnston. He and his family had lived for generations in Virginia, but this story of his life did not commence in Virginia. It commenced away across the seas, beneath a thatch-roofed cottage on the shores of the Solway Firth in Scotland. All true biography commences with genealogy. If John was the greatest man who ever lived, this is the first thing we want to know about him. Who was his father? Who was his mother? Of what race and stock did he come? What were the streams which contributed to the river of this great life? Luke, who is always the explicit and careful historian, lays great stress on this fact. He says: "There was a certain priest named Zacharias, and his wife of the daughters of Aaron, and her name was Elisabeth; and they were both righteous in the sight of the Lord."

In a letter in which he stated his qualifications for a position as tutor for which he was applying, Carlyle wrote: "Not forgetting among my other advantages the prayers of religious parents, a blessing which, if I speak less of it, I do not feel less than he." It is a blessed thing to have had a godly father, whose example is still with you, and a blessed thing to have had a pious mother, whose prayers and whose love still attend you. But it is a yet more blessed thing, a still greater responsibility, to have had a father and mother who were both "righteous in the sight of the Lord," and into whose dear, pure, calm, overcoming faces you can look in any hour of danger when life would frighten you with its tragedy, or when temptation would lure you from the path of truth and duty, whose voices call to you even from their graves and bid you hold fast to God and do the right at every cost.

Born of such parents, from the day that he was able to think,

John was taught to deny himself: "He shall be great in the sight of the Lord, and shall drink no wine nor strong drink from his mother's womb."

John's rude garments of skins and camel hair, and his diet of locusts and wild honey, did not make him great, but it is worth while noting that luxury and self-indulgence had no place in the training of the man whom Christ was to call the greatest of the sons of men. He whose preaching is to condemn the world must himself have given no pledges to the world. We frequently speak of a good environment for our children and our young people, and by it we generally mean "all the opportunities which money can buy, little responsibility, and none of the self-discipline which reveals the hidden powers and which alone should be counted a good environment."

SHAPED IN SOLITUDE

After his training in that home of piety and self-denial, John was trained in the desert. "He was in the desert until the day of his showing unto Israel." John's character was shaped in solitude. He retired from the face of man that he might see more clearly the face of God. "No man," said Thomas De Quincey, "will ever unfold the capacities of his intellect who does not at least checker his life with solitude." In the solitude of the desert, in the midst of a great physical loneliness, John learned to meet and endure that moral loneliness which men fear above all else and yet which must so often be the lot of God's true servants. Think of this greatest of all preachers and prophets, with only the Dead Sea and the undulating desert for his seminary, and with the ruins of Sodom and Gomorrah for his illuminated text, waiting until the thought of God, the grandest thought which can take possession of mortal man, took hold of him:

> I think he had not heard of the far towns,
> Nor of the dreams of men, nor of king's crowns,
> Until the thought of God took hold of him
> And he was sitting dreaming in the calm
> Of the first noon upon the desert's rim.
>
> —*Fitzgerald*

We have seen the source of John's greatness. Now what was that greatness? How did it express itself?

A GREAT CONVICTION

1. *The greatness of conviction.* There has never been a great life, a great witness, without a great conviction back of it. John was no agnostic, telling the world what he was not sure of, or what he could not believe, but with terrible earnestness he told the world what he did believe. It is the lack of conviction that threatens to kill preaching in the Protestant pulpit. What we need is not more knowledge, organization, paraphernalia, but more bed-rock conviction as to a few great facts. John had a few tremendous convictions—that the kindgom of God was at hand, that men must repent of their sins, that the Christ was at hand, and, when he saw Him, that Jesus was the Christ. With these convictions he shook the world.

That deep conviction made John sincere and earnest in his preaching. He was a burning and a shining light. The light shone because it burned. Nothing can ever take the place of that sincerity which is born of conviction. We can respect sincere men however much we differ with them, but the most gifted of men forfeits our respect if he does not ring true. What is the difference, for instance, between two men like John the Baptist and Francis Bacon? Both were sons of genius. What would a man not give to have written the essay on Truth—"What is truth, said jesting Pilate, and did not wait for the answer" or the essay on Death—"Men dread death as children fear to go in the dark!" Yet between those two men there yawns the gulf which stretches between sincerity and insincerity. "He chose," writes Bacon's biographer of him, "to please men and not to follow what his soul must have told him was the better way. He wanted in his dealings with men that sincerity upon which he so strongly insisted in his dealings with nature, and the mind of a great life was the consequence."

A GREAT HUMILITY

2. *The greatness of humility.* When John's disciples, jealous of the growing fame of Jesus, went to him in alarm and said, "Rabbi,

the same baptizeth and all men come unto Him," instead of fanning their discontent, John gave them his great answer: "The friend of the bridegroom rejoiceth greatly because of the bridegroom's voice: He must increase but I must decrease."

It is not pleasant to be told that someone can write or sing or preach or administer better than we can. We would just as soon be told something else. John never turned his own immense popularity to a selfish purpose. When his preaching was creating such a sensation, the priests and Levites sent a deputation out to interview him. They said to him, "Art thou the Christ?" "No." "Art thou Elijah?" "No." "Art thou one of the prophets? If not, who art thou? What shall we say to them that sent us? What explanation shall we give of these extraordinary scenes?"

John might have claimed any of these titles and the multitudes would have gone with him. He could have founded a new religion or set up a new government. But the friend of the bridegroom was true to the bridegroom: "Tell your masters I am only a voice crying in the wilderness. Who I am makes no difference." When Wendell Phillips stood by the open grave of John Brown on the mountaintop in the Adirondacks, he said, "How some men struggle into oblivion and others forget themselves into immortality!" Most men think too much of "who" and not enough of "what." Not far from Winchester in the Shenandoah Valley, that starlit abbey of the Confederacy, there is a monument to Virginia's unknown dead. It bears this inscription: "Who they were none know—what they were all know."

A GREAT COURAGE

3. *The greatness of courage.* The world does not commonly associate humility and courage. It likes to listen to the man who gives himself out to be somewhat and it discounts the humble man. Yet how often, when it comes to taking a stand for principle, and enduring the taunts and ridicule of the people, it is the meek and unassuming man who surprises us with the greatness of his courage. In some pathway through a deep glen of the forest you have come upon a jutting rock, covered with green moss, and through it there trickles a tiny cascade. Nothing on earth is softer than that moss, but when you tear away the moss you come upon the cold,

naked rock. So underneath John's humility was the cold, naked, adamantine rock of incorruptible and indomitable courage. Let us see how he used that courage:

The multitude flocked out to hear him and to see him, the crowds whose warm flattery has ruined so many preachers and prophets. But to them John said, "Repent! for the kingdom of heaven is at hand." Then came the publicans, the clever politicians and manipulators of the day: "Exact no more than that which is appointed you"; and after the publicans came the soldiers, the men who could overturn the government of a province in a day, no doubt attracted by this great voice and saying to themselves, "With John for our leader what could we not do, what could we not conquer!" "Master, what shall we do?" And like the ring of one of their own short swords upon the helmet of a foe came back the answer: "Do violence to no man, neither accuse any falsely; and be content with your wages."

Last of all in this strange procession to the Jordan came the Pharisees and the Sadducees, an odd alliance—the Pharisees, who by the minutia of their literality had almost choked the wells of Old Testament inspiration, and the proud Sadducees, rationalists and materialists, the modernists of their day, who disbelieved in angel and in spirit and looked with pity upon the ignorant rabble who could receive such a doctrine as the resurrection of the body. Yet these classes came to John, John of all men, and said, "Master, what shall we do?"

That was John's great test. Did he truckle to them? Did he say, "I speak in my rough, denunciatory way to the common people, but with you, of course, it is a different matter. You represent the thinking and educated classes, and even if truth must be silenced or surrendered I must hold your favor and your patronage"?

Was that the way John talked to these men? No, not that, but this: "Who hath warned you to flee from the wrath to come? Bring forth, therefore, fruits meet for repentance, and then come here to the Jordan and I will baptize you."

But there is one thing yet braver in John's preaching. It takes little courage to stand upon a platform and denounce at long range the sins of what we call "high society." It took real courage to do what John did. He marched into the palace itself and there, in the presence of the adulterous pair, said to Herod, "It is not

lawful for thee to have her; you are breaking God's commandment and God will judge you."

That sermon cost John his life. Oh, if John had been mobbed
by the people, assassinated by the soldiers, or torn by a wild beast
in the midst of one of his desert reveries, that, we think, had been
a death in keeping with his life. But to think that he had to die at
the whispered wish of a vindictive adulteress! The greatest man
who ever lived, and here is his head on a silver charger to please
the whim of a half-naked dancing girl and her angry mother! And
the sun still smiles, the earth does not yawn to swallow up the
authors of this infamy!

But wait! The evangelist tells us that when John was dead his
disciples came and took up the body and buried it, and went and
told Jesus. John had friends, disciples, and I have no doubt that
they wrapped his body in as clean a linen cloth as that which
enwound the body of the Lord, and women anointed him with
their tears. Perhaps in Jerusalem they buried the body, perhaps by
Jordan's flood, and rolled a great stone to the door of the sepulcher and departed. "It" not "him," the body, not John! They
could not bury John. Time has not been able to bury him, the
ages have not been able to engulf him. No wonder guilty Herod,
when he heard of the preaching of Jesus, stricken in conscience,
cried out in fear and remorse, "John whom I beheaded is risen
from the dead!" The soul of John the Baptist marches on, still
cries his voice in the wilderness. Every word that he uttered a
battle, and his name like an army with banners!

A GREAT MESSAGE

4. *The greatness of his message.* Shortly before His passion, Jesus
went back to the Jordan country where He had been baptized by
John and by the Holy Spirit. The disciples of John, now dead,
gathered about Him and listened to Him and saw His miracles.
This was their verdict, "John did no miracles." He never stilled
the tempest, nor opened the blind eyes, nor raised the dead—"but
all things that John spake of this man were true."

What was it that John said about Jesus? Did he say, "Behold the
man who did no sin and whose blameless life will leave the world a
great example of how to live"? Did he say, "Behold the man, the

carpenter's son who never wrote a line save in the dust, and yet the man whose words have done more to temper and soften and regenerate mankind than all the sayings of the philosophers and all the books of the ages"? Did he say, "Behold the man whose birth will be the watershed of history, dividing it into two parts, Before Christ and After Christ"? Did he say, "Behold the man whose life shall be a fountain of compassion whence shall flow the healing streams of mercy and pity"? Did he say, "Behold the man who was in the world and yet not of it and who more than any other has brought life and immortality to life"? Did he say, "Behold the man whose death on the Cross will be the supreme example of that vicarious suffering which runs like a scarlet thread through all creation"? Was that what John said of Jesus? If so, oblivion's sea had long ago swept over him. No, not that, but this, this which takes all that in, this which left out, Christianity is left out: "Behold, the Lamb of God that taketh away the sin of the world!"

It is that witness of John to Jesus that men today are trying to muffle and silence. The world will let you talk about Jesus as beautifully as you please. It will let you heap high the flowers of your eulogia, but there is one thing that the world cannot tolerate, and this is that you should say of Jesus what John said, "Behold, the Lamb of God that taketh away the sin of the world," God's eternal sacrifice for sin. Utter these words and you will find that the Cross still has ancient offense. Leave them out and you will find that then has the offense of the Cross ceased. This is the question before the Church today: Shall the offense of the Cross cease? Shall the Gospel cease to be good news and become only good advice? Shall the Churches which have been entrusted with the Gospel become lighthouses whose light has been quenched, or, still worse, lighthouses which burn and flash with false lights which allure to destruction voyagers on the sea of life?

"Behold, the Lamb of God that taketh away the sin of the world!" Wherever that is left out Christianity is left out. Wherever it is spoken and honored there the Gospel is preached, whether from the incense-laden altars of Greek and Roman Churches or in the severe dignity of our Reformed Churches, or in a Gospel mission, or to the accompaniment of a bass drum on the street, or when at eventide a mother tells her little child of the love of God in Christ. Man is still a sinner, and still his great need is redemption from sin. Calvary has no successor; the Lamb of God has no substitute. He is the sinner's only hope. He is the power and glory of the Church here, and hereafter He is the Lamb of God, no longer upon the Cross but upon the throne of the universe, to whom redeemed sinners will pay their grateful homage.

"And I saw and heard a voice of many angels round about the throne, and the number of them was ten thousand times ten thousand, and thousands of thousands, saying with a great voice: Worthy is the Lamb which hath been slain to receive power, and riches, and wisdom, and might, and honor, and glory, and blessing. And every created thing which is in the heaven and on the earth and under the earth and on the sea, and all things that are therein, heard I saying: Blessing, and honor, and glory, and power, be unto Him that sitteth upon the throne, and unto the Lamb for ever and ever, Amen."

QUESTIONS FOR DISCUSSION

CHAPTER 1

1. Think about and discuss the special problems connected with sharing your faith with a sibling. A workmate. A chance acquaintance.
2. On page 17 Macartney says: "Many, if not all, of our problems in the church today stem from a 'lack of Andrew's brother-seeking spirit.'" Do you agree?
3. What activities in your church could be given up in pursuit of "more Andrews"?
4. Read the quote from *The Last Days of Pompeii*. Compare this to the definition of evangelism: "Evangelism is one beggar telling another where to find bread."
5. What is the "fruit that should remain" to which Jesus referred in John 15:16?

CHAPTER 2

1. On page 22 Macartney mentions those "churchified" Christians who have lost all contact with people outside the church, "who are so heavenly minded that they are no earthly good." Is this a problem in the church today—in *your* church?
2. Is there any significance, do you think, in the fact that Philip first took the visiting Greeks to Andrew—and then the two took them to Jesus? What does this tell you about Andrew? About Philip?
3. Think about and discuss the implication of Philip's simple

137

invitation, "come and see." How does this apply to Christian witness today?

4. Using a Bible dictionary or concordance, look up all the Scripture references to Philip. What kind of man emerges from this research?

CHAPTER 3

1. Why, do you suppose, did Matthew describe himself as the "publican"? To what vocation today would you compare his work?

2. Study the poem on page 28. What kind of man do you think Matthew was?

3. What prior contact, if any, do you think Matthew had experienced with Jesus?

4. On page 29 Macartney implies, "Matthew is thus to be distinguished among the Twelve as the man in whom already Christ, before the period of training, had wrought a profound transformation." Matthew's conversion could almost be described as cataclysmic. As Macartney says: "For him to leave the lucrative business of the tax collector and join himself to the wandering disciples of Jesus meant a profound moral change, a mighty upheaval in his soul. For this reason Matthew in his very call was a type of the moral transformation which Christ is able to effect in men's lives. By calling Matthew to follow him, Jesus showed that He was able to save even to the uttermost all who come unto Him."

5. On page 31 the author says that "Matthew, finally, is a type of conservative." Read the rest of his evaluation of Matthew. Does this expansion on the biblical context open any new windows of understanding for you?

CHAPTER 4

1. On page 33 Macartney points out that "the tax collector (Matthew) and the tax hater (Simon) both followed Jesus." Explore the ramifications of this contrast in converts to Christ— two men from opposite ends of the spectrum. Can you think of other "extremists" who have come to Christ? Discuss.

2. A. B. Bruce, in contrasting Jesus and Simon, said, "One (Simon) had recourse to carnal weapons of war, the sword and the dagger;

the other relied solely on the gentle but omnipotent force of truth." Do you feel this contrast is justified? Could it be said of other followers of Jesus?

3. Simon, says Macartney, is "transformed from the Hebrew patriot to the Christian patriot" (see page 36). Just what, do you think, was involved in that transformation? Can you think of more modern illustrations of this kind of drastic change?

4. Read the description of Christians on pages 36 and 37. Does this same hold true for Christians today? Was Simon that kind of Christian?

CHAPTER 5

1. Macartney likens "James the Less" to a bridge builder and a "tree planter"—A Christian who is content to work behind the scenes without outward recognition. He also compares him to a soldier content to serve in the ranks without an officer's elevation and the recognition that comes with such prominence. Where do you think the church would be without these kinds of "unsung heroes"?

2. Macartney quotes 1 Samuel 30:24 in placing James the Less among those who "stand by the stuff" rather than fighting for David in the front lines. Can you think of people who "stand by the stuff" in your church? In your wider acquaintance?

3. On page 43 Macartney says of James the Less: " . . . still in his history and service as an apostle of the Lord Jesus Christ we have an example of a pure and altogether disinterested service for Christ. That is what will make good workmen of us all, to be impressed with the majesty of Jesus, the supremacy of the kingdom of God, and the eternal worthwhileness of contributing our share to the advancement of the Kingdom." What would happen in your church if everyone took that kind of selfless attitude toward their service?

CHAPTER 6

1. This Judas (not Iscariot) is known only as the disciple who asked, "Lord, how is it that You will reveal Yourself—make Yourself real—to us and not to the world?" (John 14:22, Amplified). What does this question suggest to you about the personality of this "shadowy" disciple? Can you identify with his concern?

2. Compare Judas' question to that of Philip given earlier in the chapter. And also to that of Thomas. Were they all asking somewhat the same question?

3. Summarize Jesus' answer beginning in verse 23. Read it in several translations and then put it in your own words.

4. On page 48 Macartney says, "The disciples may see Jesus when the world does not." Read the rest of that paragraph and discuss particularly the author's conclusions expressed in the last sentence, beginning "If your Christian faith is not strong enough. . . ." Compare what he says to what Job endured. How did Job survive his testing? What can you learn from him?

CHAPTER 7

1. Macartney, along with most commentators, says that Bartholomew and Nathaniel are one and the same, which is why this book does not have a separate chapter on Nathaniel. In any event, Macartney classifies Bartholomew as skeptical or prejudiced, citing his question in John 1:46, "Can any good thing come out of Nazareth?" Bartholomew, if nothing else, says Macartney was guileless, a man of integrity. With him, "what you saw is what you got."

2. Keeping in mind Bartholomew's open-mindedness (see page 53), study his answer to Jesus, "Thou art the Son of God, Thou art the King of Israel" (John 1:49). Probe this reply and try to learn more about Bartholomew's (Nathaniel's) personality from it. Construct a character sketch based on your conclusions.

3. Discuss the implications of the statement, " . . . in Christ men discover their true spiritual homeland" (page 55).

CHAPTER 8

1. Reread Tennyson's lines on page 57. Do you agree that Thomas is an example or illustration of the truth proclaimed in this poem?

2. How do you explain Thomas's courage expressed in John 11:6 ("Let us also go that we may die with Him") and his doubt (with which we usually associate him) when told of the risen Christ?

3. On page 59 Macartney says, "The difference between the rationalist and Thomas is this: the rationalist wants to disbelieve; Thomas wanted to believe. The rationalist, of the honest type, is

occasioned by study, by examination of evidence, by the pressing bounds of the natural world, making the other world seem unreal; but the doubt of Thomas was the doubt born of sorrow." What does he mean "this is the deepest doubt of all"?

4. "Things troubled Thomas that did not trouble the other disciples," says Macartney on page 61. Why do you think Thomas was different from the rest? Read a biographical sketch of Thomas in one or more Bible dictionaries and discuss.

CHAPTER 9

1. Why, do you think, Jesus had special regard for John?

2. What does this special relationship tell you about Jesus?

3. Compare John's personality (as a "son of thunder") in his youth to his personality as an old man. What does this tell you about the effect of aging on some personalities and not on others?

4. It is the other evangelists (Matthew, Mark and Luke) who mention John's so-called "failures." What does that tell you about John? Think of his tenderness and contrast it with his toughness. Do you know any Christians like that?

5. What does Macartney mean when he says, "When John writes, the first blush of the Christian enthusiasm has commenced to fade and the age of interpretation and theology has commenced"? Do you agree?

CHAPTER 10

1. James was the first apostle to die—not the first martyr. What does this suggest about his witness and work? As the elder brother of John, what kind of personality do you think he had?

2. John and James shared the same mother—Salome—and it is interesting to speculate the kind of mother she was, to have borne two such strong sons. Do you agree with Macartney's evaluation of her?

3. James and John also shared the same father—Zebedee— and could have inherited their "power personalities" from him. In the light of what you know about both sons, which of the two parents do you think had the most influence in their lives?

4. Read the story of "Abraham's visitor" on page 80. Do you agree with Macartney's conclusion?

5. Do you agree with his comments on the positive aspects of anger on pages 81 and 82?

CHAPTER 11

1. Macartney calls Peter "the most human of all the apostles." Do you feel that way about him?

2. On page 84 Macartney divides personalities into four types: that of Thomas, James, John, and Peter— and he calls Peter "impulsive, affectionate, ready in speech, enthusiastic, sometimes boastful, but strong-hearted and strong-minded." He also attracted many to him, making him a natural leader. Why do you suppose Peter stands out from among the other disciples so strikingly?

3. On page 86 Macartney says, "Peter was not an average two-talent man." Read the rest of his characterization. What trait of Peter's most stands out for you? Why?

4. Study the accusations of Peter's inconsistency made by Macartney in this chapter. How would you defend him—or would you?

5. As a "sinner saved by grace," Peter lived long enough to be called a "saint." What could account for this phenomenal growth?

CHAPTER 12

1. From a saint, we now proceed to study an almost "satanic" person—Judas Iscariot. He is probably the most mysterious character in the Bible—certainly the most complex of all the disciples. In most Bible dictionaries little is said of the other men named Judas who are mentioned, but much is usually said about this traitor. How would you describe his "remorse" or "repentance"? Why wasn't it sufficient to restore his fellowship with Christ?

2. How did you feel about Judas before you read this chapter? Was he more a traitor—or more a trickster? How do you feel now?

3. How could such a man become "one of the twelve"? Discuss.

4. What do you think were the motives of Judas in betraying the Christ?

5. What do you think is meant by the statement, "Satan entered into him"?

6. Read the poem on page 101. React to its message.

CHAPTER 13

1. Church history "is the history of waiting" says Macartney on page 104. What does this say to our Christian world today in terms of its attitude toward world events?

2. All we know of Matthias is his name— and yet he was considered qualified to become one of the "chosen twelve" (Acts 1:21-26). Read through the qualifications listed by Peter in a modern translation. What qualifications would you have added, if any? Is this a valid guide for the church today in its search for suitable leadership?

3. "What right have these nobodies to stand for the high office of the apostolate?" Macartney asks. "They had the right of faith and character and fidelity. Ordinarily, in political affairs today, one of the qualifications for a candidate with the people is that they should have heard much about him. But for every candidate of whom we have heard much there are thousands upon thousands of whom we have heard nothing, who are just as well, perhaps better, qualified to hold the office in question." How does this same problem impact the church as a whole today? Your church?

4. On page 108 Macartney says: "The havoc wrought by sin will be undone; the place of the son of perdition will be taken by the son of prayer." He goes on to apply this to the perfection of the church "carried out in its individual members." What does that truth say to us in the church today?

CHAPTER 14

1. Beginning with this chapter, the author seeks to discuss men who were not members of the original apostolate. React to Macartney's justification for the inclusion of these early followers in this book.

2. How do you feel about Macartney's contemplation of the relationship of Jesus and James (see page 112)? What additional questions would you ask?

3. Why did Jesus' brethren (and indeed, His other followers) have such a problem understanding His spiritual kingdom?

4. How do you react to the idea that sibling jealousy existed in Jesus' family?

CHAPTER 15

1. On page 120 Macartney says, " . . . there is much in Paul which is capable of imitation and where humble Christians can follow him." He then cites: His self-image and appreciation of human nature. His love for others. His heroism.

   Reread this section and apply it to everyday Christian life today.

2. Discuss the four elements of Paul's life which Macartney lists on pages 123 to 125 and answer the following questions:

   A. What hints do we have in Paul's life and writings as to his concern for self?

   B. Read a selection of verses from Paul's writings and discuss his motivation: Rom. 9:3; 1 Cor. 13; 2 Tim. 4:5-8; Gal. 5:22-26; 1 Tim. 6:10-14.

   C. Read 1 Thessalonians 3:15—13 and other Pauline passages in which he talks about his personal relationship with Christ and discuss. Reread the poem on page 125 and apply it to Paul.

   D. Think about some of the people whom Paul befriended and discuss the ingredients of true friendship.

CHAPTER 16

1. Read John 1:6—8, 15—21. Based on these verses, discuss the reason(s) for the greatness of John the Baptist.

2. Read the section, "Shaped in Solitude," and discuss the lessons in loneliness which men like John, Moses, David, etc. learned while alone with God.

3. Macartney lists four ways in which John's greatness expressed itself. Look at the greatness of each of the following: his convictions, his humility, his courage, his message and discuss.

4. Compare John the Baptist and Paul and discuss their similarities and their differences.